Ted Polhemus is a social anthropologist who, for more than twenty years, has explored all aspects of popular culture. His books include *Fashion and Anti-Fashion*, *Popstyles* and *Bodystyles*. He is also a photographer, a teacher, an exhibition organizer, a marketing consultant and a frequent guest on television and radio.

Housk Randall was born in La Mesa, California, to a Mexican mother and a Welsh/Cherokee father. Since childhood he has been a composer and musician. At the age of thirty-three Housk was found to have cancer of the throat. During his treatment and recuperation he found and fell in love with photography. *Rituals of Love* is his second book; his first is *Revelations: Chronicles and Visions from the Sexual Underworld*. Housk was awarded the first 'Oscar' for Best Erotic Photographer US/UK in the 1994 'Erotic Oscars'.

RITUALS OF LOVE

Sexual Experiments, Erotic Possibilities

TED POLHEMUS and **HOUSK RANDALL**

PICADOR

First published 1994 by Picador

a division of Pan Macmillan Publishers Limited
Cavaye Place London SW10 9PG
and Basingstoke

Associated companies throughout the world

ISBN 0 330 33093 4

9 8 7 6 5 4 3 2 1

A CIP catalogue record for this book is available from the British Library

Typeset by Parker Typesetting Service, Leicester
Printed and bound in Great Britain by
BPC Hazell Books Ltd
A member of
The British Printing Company Ltd

For Betti and Jane

CONTENTS

ACKNOWLEDGEMENTS

Ted Polhemus and Housk Randall would like to thank:

All those who allowed themselves to be photographed and interviewed, our editor Georgia Garrett, Isabel Kaprowski, Tuppy Owens, Henry and Lynn Ferguson of *Body Art* magazine, Patrick Gilson of Catalogue Connection, Skin Two, Pandora Gorey and Andy Harrison, Nicola Joly, Debbie Pickford, Janette Rozing, Nicky Mcelwaine, Natalie Bishop-Lemercier, Patricia Morrison, Ray & Rosie, Sarah Tierney, Steve & Sadie of Westward Bound, Ron & Paul of Chain Gang Promotions, Dave & Alan of The Torture Garden, Kaizu & Louiza, Claude & Velda of Pagan Metal, Sarah Lloyd at Ilford Anitec Ltd.

All photographic materials supplied by Ilford Anitec Ltd.

RITUALS
OF
LOVE

HOT MONOGAMY

What is sex? Back in the sixties when I was a teenager such a question would have seemed absurd – you either did *it* or you didn't. There was foreplay of course but, as its name suggests, it was a means to an end, not the Real Thing. The sixties definition of sex was as simple as it was obvious: *It* = intercourse, genital penetration to orgasm (at least for the male). The only thing that was seen as problematic was getting there.

The question 'What is sex?' seems to me today, middle-aged in the nineties, both fascinating and critical. Is this shift from the ridiculous to the sublime simply a product of middle-age and its tendency to contemplation? Certainly in part. But not completely, because I'm not the only element in the equation that has changed: 'What is sex?' is a nineties sort of question because as I've grown older and more complicated so has the world I live in.

What turns people on has always been subjective (a fact of life that was recognized even in the simplistic sixties), but increasingly what is/isn't 'sex' is defined much more personally and idiosyncratically. The *meaning* of sex itself is changing – broadening, expanding and becoming less distinct. If you were to ask any of the people whose photographs and interviews appear in this book 'Did you do *it* last night?', aside from getting some pretty strange looks, an answer would only be forthcoming once you had defined your terms more precisely.

These people are members of what has come to be known as 'the Fetish Scene', 'the S/M Scene' or simply 'the Scene'. They probably wouldn't see themselves – and certainly would not be seen by the majority – as typical representatives of the nineties, yet their erotic experiments do reflect mass preoccupations. They are at the cutting edge of a radical expansion and reappraisal of the sexual territory. For some, that which might previously have been seen only as an appetizer has been reclassified as a satisfying main course. For others, every item on the menu has been completely changed, with all manner of exotic concoctions replacing the traditional fare. And at the risk of extending this culinary metaphor too far, there are even those who are sated by simply perusing the menu.

The Scene states explicitly an idea that is gradually being acknowledged by mainstream society: that sex ain't what it used to be. Sex today can be whatever you want it to be: dressing up, role-playing, mutual masturbation, solo masturbation, various oral activities, exhibitionism, voyeurism, fetishism, bondage, S/M . . . or just thinking about sex. (For if the sixties, in a kind of inverse puritanism, insisted 'Don't dream it, do it,' today's world has grown more appreciative of the value of fantasy.) Of course, none of the activities listed above are recent inventions; what is perhaps uniquely contemporary is a disinclination to distinguish between means ('foreplay') and ends ('it') and a post-modern, eclectic inclination to throw everything together into one bubbling pot of polymorphous 'perversity'.

All of which is good news for those who, concerned with the spread of AIDS, advocate non-penetrative sexual strategies (and, as we shall consider in a moment, 'Scene sex' can be seen at least in part as a response to AIDS' dark shadow). But this new sexual revolution is also very confusing. What once seemed straightforward has become an enigma. Even our vocabulary is in a state of flux. Words fail us (and in an age increasingly obsessed with *talking* about sex there is more than a little irony in this).

It seems that *sex* – its defining limits and its inter-personal objectivity shot to hell – teeters on the brink of becoming a meaningless word; signifying everything and meaning nothing. Likewise *pleasure*, so handy a word in the 'If it feels good, do it' sixties, becomes more problematic in the context of whips and nipple clamps. And what about *love*? Like 'God', 'love' has always been an impossible word to slot succinctly into a dictionary but it was easier to *think* you could define it in the context of a hippy commune than it is in the context of an S/M dungeon.

Words aren't everything but you know that something is happening in a culture when their meanings implode or their connotations suddenly flip upside-down. Negro→black, chick→woman, homosexual→gay all signalled important social transformations, while 'queer' and even 'nigger' are words now in the process of being reclaimed with irony and defiance by those who have had to suffer them as terms of abuse. Of particular relevance to this book is the way in which the word 'pervert' is switching from critical abuse to righteous, in-your-face affirmation. Most, if not all, of the people in this book are proud to be *pervs*, happily embracing a terminology that mainstream society continues to spit out with disdain.

Language always lags behind visual symbols and one need only look at today's fashion, advertising or pop videos to realize that perviness pervades the mass as well as the minority. Everywhere you look (and this is as true of continental Europe, Japan and the USA as it is of Britain), that which excites is that which incorporates some undercurrent of erotic weirdness, decadence, perversity. The erotic, like everything else, is subject to fashion change – the pendulum swinging between nature and artifice, sunlight and darkness, normality and deviance, the girl/boy next door and the vampiric alien other. (These contrasts are all perfectly realized in David Lynch's film *Blue Velvet*.)

There can be little question of which side of the pendulum's swing we are on today. Some have sought to explain this state of affairs by pointing to the *fin de siècle* phenomenon: the idea that whenever history approaches the end of one century and the beginning of another, sexual attitudes and experience get a bit strange. Certainly this was true of Toulouse-Lautrec's Paris and Freud's Vienna in the final years of the last century. And, to a certain extent, parallels could be drawn with the period of moral and ideological ferment which characterized the era of the French Revolution at the close of the eighteenth century.

All of which makes for very neat and tidy theorizing, but it is difficult to see what possible mechanisms might exist to trigger this process. Do people really say to themselves 'Well, I see the century is drawing to a close so we'd better start getting decadent.'? Simple coincidence seems a more likely bet to me. While there may be insights to be gained from examining the fetishistic inclinations of the 1890s, the fact of the matter is that history never really repeats itself.

The sexual is always a distillation of everything that is going on in a culture. The world today is very different from the 1890s – economically, technologically, socially, ideologically, aesthetically. And erotically. Like them or loathe them, our perversities are our own – a précis of the world we inhabit.

Café Flesh is a cult film that visualizes a time in the future when the vast majority of people are 'sex negatives' – people who become ill when they attempt to have sex but who find a kind of fulfilment in going to places like the Café Flesh of the title to watch the few remaining 'sex positives' pleasuring themselves. Like all good exercises in futurology, *Café Flesh* reflects a present-day reality.

Our world is in the midst of a sexual crisis. While few people may exhibit the extreme symptoms of the 'sex negatives' of *Café Flesh*, it is clear – for example from the letters to the agony aunts of popular magazines – that a huge gap exists between erotic expectations and sexual realities.

There is in our society a worryingly high proportion of people suffering from impotence, frigidity and other medically recognized sexual dysfunctions. But there are also many less definable problems that are ultimately just as worrying and just as indicative of this crisis: there is what might be called 'fantasy collapse', when the rug is pulled out from beneath those dreams that normally energize our lives; there is what some have termed 'sexual addiction', which is characterized by an ever-restless, frantic search for something – anything – to make the earth move; but, most of all, there is simply widespread dissatisfaction with our own sexual experiences, which somehow never seem to live up to our culture's extravagant myths of erotic fulfilment. ('It is the ghost of desire that haunts the defunct reality of sex. Sex is everywhere, except in sexuality.' Jean Baudrillard, *Seduction*[1])

Add all of this together, and the scope of our contemporary sexual crisis becomes all too evident. If we were to define a 'sex negative' as a person who can't seem to bridge the gap between expectation and reality, then *Café Flesh* is more like a documentary than a futuristic fantasy. As in the paintings by George Grosz in Berlin between the wars, our contemporary world oozes with what Baudrillard so aptly terms 'the ghost of desire', yet satisfaction seems to be in short supply. Everywhere you look there is erotic titillation – and an undercurrent of sexual dis-ease.

I'm old enough to remember when sexual satisfaction was, if not guaranteed, at least something you felt sure was lurking round the next corner. Back in the sixties one lived in hope. The Age of Aquarius would usher in a world without inhibitions, a world of unlimited sexual possibility, a world of tensions released, dreams fulfilled. Next stop: full frontal, sexually explicit, two girls for every boy, two boys for every girl, nirvana.

What a bummer, therefore, to find yourself instead in *Café Flesh*.

Of course today, in retrospect, one doesn't have to be especially perceptive to see that *Café Flesh* has grown from the premiss of an inherently dodgy nirvana. In the rest of this chapter we will consider the legacy of the sixties' 'Sexual Revolution' in more detail; briefly (and obviously), the game plan of this revolution left a lot to be desired *because the liberation on offer wasn't actually very liberated*.

The first problem was the way in which the sexual revolution was billed as a requisite of a larger, all-encompassing political transformation in Western society. Make no mistake; the erotic, the sexual, always reflects political realities (and even political possibilities and dreams) but it is naïve to asssume, as we hippies so often did, that one could screw one's way to a utopian society. If this faulty logic was an error of political strategy it was even more an error of sexual strategy. What might have been a pleasure became a social responsibility, an obligation.

The second problem was that the Sexual Revolution never actually got round to revolutionizing sex. When all was said and done, the sex that one was obliged to have night and day was actually pretty staid stuff. Sure, you could do it in the bath, at a pop festival, while surfing or at a love-in, but the *it* that you were doing was as proscribed as it had been in the fifties (and probably much more so than in the *1850*s). To suggest a bit of bondage to your average hippy would have been like waving a piece of raw meat at a vegan. Because the Sexual Revolution accepted no possibility of historical antecedent (and therefore enjoyed no maturity), its 'liberation' was condemned endlessly to circle the obvious: casual promiscuity.

With expectations of nirvana stoked up by media over-kill, THE SEXUAL REVOLUTION writ large became the desperate imperative of the seventies. Mr/Miss Goodbar would be found, ecstasy achieved. Long Live the Revolution. But in the end . . . singles bar clichés, lowest common denominator sex, the morning after, herpes, AIDS.

Things just didn't work out as planned. When Madonna's book *Sex* came out in 1992 she was interviewed by Andrew Neil, editor of the *Sunday Times*, who asked her: 'Didn't we go through that sexual revolution in the sixties?' and then persisted: 'But your argument still draws heavily on the sixties' 'anything goes' approach.'[2]

But did 'anything go' in the sixties? Certainly my hippy friends would have rejected Madonna and practically every page of her book as 'unnatural', 'plastic', 'gross', 'sick', and, most of all, 'unliberated'. To my eyes, the sort of 'Scene sex' which Madonna's book catalogues embodies a completely different approach to sexuality from that proposed in the sixties. Chalk and cheese. Yet in Andrew Neil's eyes there is simply an unbroken continuum.

And he is not alone. Even Madonna in her replies to his questions cannot seem to step outside the presumption that the sixties defined 'liberation', and hence its failure, for all time. It is for this reason that we must put on our flares or mini-skirts and journey back again to the decade that refuses to die.

Every generation thinks that it has invented sex and in a sense this is true. Rather than being a fixed *thing*, sex is a set of meanings and expectations which are generated within a given place and time. Usually, however, this new take on sexuality remains a secret shared within the generation that devised it, only much later taking its place within the entire culture's system of erotic meanings. In the 1960s, however, things worked out differently.

To understand anything about what has happened in the West since the Second World War it is necessary to take on board a simple demographic fact: my generation, the Baby Boomers, constitutes a huge statistical blip which has at each stage of its life cycle – like a black hole – drawn the rest of Western culture into its gravitational field. The simple fact that there were so many of us gave us inordinate consumer power; everyone else had to kowtow to our youthful whims and inclinations. The eventual result of this was the youthification of our entire culture – including the erotic.

When, in the course of the 1960s, my generation came of age sexually, and, like all generations, put our own twist on sexual meaning, a sexual revolution sizzled through every nook and cranny of our culture. This extrapolating of one generation's sexual awakening into an entire culture's sexuality had precisely the effect one would expect: it gave Western sexuality both the vitality and the naïvety of adolescent desires.

While the Youth Revolution and the Sexual Revolution of the sixties were one and the same thing (inevitably so because of simple demographics) their impact was compounded by a range of other social and cultural factors. Science gave us the pill and, coupled with penicillin, this appeared to render promiscuity a safe pursuit. Leisure time and prosperity (together with the fact that many more women now worked outside the home) created an arena of opportunity. Social and geographic mobility enabled everyone to come to the party. And the decline of religious beliefs weakened the moral impediments to the logical imperative of liberation.

How could all of this have not resulted in a sexual revolution? In fact, there were *several* sexual revolutions in the sixties – each with its own distinctive characteristics and yet, thirty years on, they all seem strangely similar.

There was the '*Playboy* magazine sexual revolution' in America which coincided with (and often interfaced with) the 'Swinging sixties sexual revolution' in Britain. Both of these had roots in the late fifties but established a dominating cultural presence in the early sixties. Both left much to be desired from a feminist perspective. Both sought to celebrate the fusion of sexual promiscuity with affluent capitalism and both hankered after some groovy, sci-fi future when inhibitions would be a thing of the past. *Barbarella*, James Bond movies, *Blow Up*, Mary Quant, Pierre Cardin, David Bailey, Christine Keeler, Mandy Rice-Davies, *The Avengers* and an ever-growing army of *Playboy* bunnies provided the images for this triumph of libidinal capitalism (now available only in Japan).

The 'hippy sexual revolution' came on stream in any significant mass media sense (and when it comes to sexual revolutions nothing else matters) only in the latter half of the sixties. In many ways this event marked a complete break with the brave new world forged earlier in the decade. For while the presumption that 'He who has the flashiest sports car will pull the most birds/bunnies' had been central to the *Playboy*/swinging sixties revolutions, according to the tenets of the hippy sexual revolution, sexual liberation and money had nothing to do with one another – *free* love was what it was all about.

Aesthetically the hippies were going down a completely different road, defining *Barbarella*-style futurism not only as unnatural but also *unsexy*. And yet when *Playboy* ran a major article on the hippy phenomenon ('The New Wave Makers', October 1967 issue), what's really striking is the ease with which the earlier sexual revolution was able to align itself with the later one. What sports-car-driving, vintage-whisky-drinking, attaché-case-carrying playboy wouldn't want to attend a 'paisley paint-in' at an 'uninhibited swinging' party in San Francisco where the curvaceous hippy girls wore flower power decorations and nothing else? And what hippy did not in his youth first perceive the possibilities of 'sexual liberation' from the pages of a well-thumbed copy of *Playboy* kept hidden in the garage or under the bed?

To see the historical inevitability of free love getting into bed with the affluent playboy swingers one can turn to Gay Talese's book *Thy Neighbour's Wife: Sex in the World Today*. In it, Talese studies the founding of the hippy communities dedicated to the exploration of late sixties-style liberation and describes how, slowly but steadily, these experiments merge into and become indistinguishable from the networks of affluent 'swingers' that had been steadily growing since the early sixties.

My point is that despite all the differences of ideology and aesthetics (precisely the sorts of thing that one would normally presume to be generative of sexual attitude) there was only *one* sexual revolution in the sixties: the sexuality defined by the Baby Boomer's youthfulness which, by definition, would be rebellious, casual, promiscuous and lacking in erotic complexity. Looked at positively, it was a sexuality full of beans and free of jaded maturity. Looked at negatively, it was bound to have a short shelf-life before boredom and dis-ease set in.

The Youth/Sexual Revolution, having danced its way through swinging London, played its way through Hugh Hefner's cascading swimming pools and tripped its way through hippy communes in California and Wales, and eventually found its ultimate haven in Plato's Retreat and other swingers' clubs where 'I'm Nick and this is Sally, would you like to make it with us?' led to great heaving piles of naked bodies pumping away to disco rhythms.

I know this because I once visited Plato's Retreat in New York. This was in the early eighties. I was intrigued, fascinated and – yes – turned on by the spectacle I saw before me. Here was the realization of the uninhibited liberation that I'd first been promised in the pages of *Playboy* and later by the hippies.

Hundreds of naked couples were at it in the Matt Room, the blue movie room, the recreation room, the restaurant, the disco, the swimming pool and the Jacuzzi. There was no aggression, much politeness. These were healthy, apparently happy, mostly physically attractive people doing their thing and in the process actualizing the 'modern' philosophy which lay at the heart of the various sexual revolutions of the sixties.

And yet somehow I also found the huffing and puffing piles of bodies a disturbing sight. Was this my puritanical background returned to haunt me as I faced the prospect of nirvana? Or was this scene of full-tilt decadence simply lacking in erotic *frisson*? Was it too like a theme park for libertines?

It would take me many years before I could trust my inclination towards the latter view.

In his book *Seduction*, the French philosopher Jean Baudrillard mounts a vibrant, no-holds-barred attack on the Sexual Revolution and its aftermath. Without a tinge of puritanism (but with the fire of an Old Testament prophet), Baudrillard castigates us for confusing 'stereo-porno' with the Real Thing.

> Nothing is less certain today than sex, behind the liberation of its discourse. And nothing today is less certain than desire, behind the proliferation of its images.[3]

> When desire is entirely on the side of demand, when it is operationalized without restrictions, it loses its imaginary and, therefore, its reality; it appears everywhere but in generalized simulation.[4]

Baudrillard's view is that in our contemporary 'frenzy of unlimited sex' we have lost everything – eroticism, desire, even, ironically, sex itself – because we have lost the *frisson* of the seductive. Like a supernova no longer able to sustain itself, our contemporary sexuality has imploded and emits no radiance because it possesses no magic, no poetry, no charm, no veiled illusion, no sorcery, no secrets and no playfulness.

How very old fashioned. How very right. In making sex more open and possible (even mandatory), we have evaporated away its power, its potential and even in any significant sense its possibility. This, then, is where the Sexual Revolution has got us.

Nowhere are the naïve and adolescent qualities of our so-called 'liberation' more evident than in its impatience with sexual/erotic tension. The keystone of Pop sex is *instant gratification* – drawing the shortest possible route between arousal and the release of the tension which that arousal generates. The analogy with fast food is obvious: satisfy the craving before it becomes an irritant. (Baudrillard's advice would presumably be to stay hungry.)

Further insight into this is provided by Tom Wolfe in his essay 'The Boiler Room and the Computer', which reminds us of the extraordinary extent to which the sexual revolution was built upon the metaphor of a human being as a boilerhouse which builds up steam (pent-up libido) that must periodically be discharged via some sort of safety valve. (This sexual model is graphically evident in the phrase 'relief massage'.) Suffering from unnecessary sexual tension? Get rid of it! Clean out your pipes! Relieve the pressure!

Thus, sex is more than recreation: it is an *anaesthetic* – a balm applied to an irritating itch. And therefore it is a sexual system which has no room, no tolerance (and not even any understanding) of that which cannot exist within the imperative of instant release – namely, the vertigo of seduction, the *frisson* of erotic tension.

'Ours is a culture of premature ejaculation,' says Baudrillard, and nowhere is this more evident than in clubs like Plato's Retreat, where orgasms are added up as scores in some sporting event. Here amongst the machinery of bodies one can see all too clearly that even 'pleasure' has come to play second fiddle to the need to release pent-up libidinal pressures.

It was during my visit to Plato's Retreat in the early eighties that I was asked if similar clubs existed in London. I replied that I didn't know of any but that a new club called Skin Two had recently opened that catered to those interested in the Fetish Scene. I enthusiastically described how those in the club often wore exotic, head-to-toe catsuits made of rubber, leather or PVC. How 'slaves' might be led around on leads attached to dog collars round their necks. I told of seeing bondage and S/M rituals, of slaves used as foot stools, of tightly laced corsets, of amazingly perilous high heels.

'But do people screw in this club?' my companions asked, while casually fondling one another.

'No,' I replied.

There was a long pause, and then, 'So why do people go there?'

At the time I could think of no suitable answer to this question but now, some ten years later, I think I've come up with one.

RIA/NYALL

HOUSK	What do you do for a living?
RIA	I'm a strippergram girl.
NYALL	I make sure Ria's safe: take her to work, wait for her and bring her home.
HOUSK	When did you first discover S/M?
RIA	I'm not quite sure how I found out but I seem to remember knowing about it from an early age. Although I was sixteen when Nyall and I started to check it out, I'd been into the clothes for quite a few years already — I've always loved rubber dresses. We started going to the parties and really seeing what could be done and that's how I discovered I liked it.
NYALL	I've always felt there was a lot more to relationships than just straight sex, even when I was a teenager. I didn't know what S/M was at the time but I was very inventive with what I wanted to do. I guess it was a natural progression from having thoughts in my head to actually finding a partner who understood and wanted to explore the same avenues, though that isn't so easy to find.

I've always felt there was a lot more to relationships than just straight sex

HOUSK	So for S/M to work for you it has to be mutual?
NYALL	Absolutely, or it's just one-sided violence. You can't explore the physical and mental side to its fullest and most satisfying extent without both partners wanting it and trusting each other. Total honesty is essential, whether you're Top or Bottom, or it doesn't work.
HOUSK	So what part does S/M play in your lives?
RIA	It's not an everyday 24-hour thing. Sometimes we'll do it when we're in bed, mostly when we socialize — almost all our friends are on the Scene.

It's always there, but not to rigorous rules, there's no specified ritual. **NYALL**

Speak for yourself, I certainly don't think about it all the time. When we're **RIA**
doing our everyday living I don't think about it. When I'm at the
supermarket I don't think about it.

Well, it's in the back of *my* mind all the time. **NYALL**

What does S/M do for you? HOUSK

It turns me on. It seems natural for me to be submissive so, although I'm **RIA**

not always in the mood for sex, I'm always ready to be submissive: 'Yes, Master, please, Master,' that kind of thing.

NYALL I think Ria's hit it on the nail; it's natural for the two of us. I don't feel like a different person when I do S/M, it's not like a power kick or pretending to be who you're not, it's just a turn-on.

RIA You see, If I'm turned on I like pain, though it doesn't feel painful, more an enjoyable sensation.

My goal is to be able to excite Ria and give her as much pleasure as I
can. She trusts me to take her to her limits of pain/pleasure and still keep
her sexually excited. I can always tell if it's just hurting or if it's painful
pleasure and that's where I get my kick, knowing her so well I can control
her body and mind for her benefit.

NYALL

What's the black box for?

HOUSK

One night we saw some friends using it and it looked like so much fun we

RIA

got one ourselves. It has glass attachments that glow purple and it gives you an electric shock that I find quite pleasant. It was originally used to stimulate sore muscles and help regenerate hair growth but the way we use it is much more fun.

HOUSK   Has S/M helped keep your relationship exciting?

RIA   Definitely. The parties and atmosphere around the Scene are openly sexual and yet you aren't pressurized into doing anything you don't want to. Nyall might let a friend spank me in public if I'm willing but sexually we're exclusive to each other. We don't mind being sexual in front of our friends but we don't include them.

The opening night of the original Skin Two club in London in November 1983 was an important occasion. Not because the outfits worn or the activities indulged in were all that remarkable. Certainly not because of the size of the event – there were probably no more than 150 of us in total. The auspiciousness of the night lay in the mix of hard-core, 'real' fetishists and trendy, young fashion types. While credit for this must go in part to the organizers (a couple who have since found fame and fortune working in other areas and who wish to remain anonymous) the fact is that Skin Two opened at precisely the right time and in precisely the right place.

Back in 1976 London had seen the first punks provocatively parading themselves in fetishistic outfits of the sort that had previously been intended only for private use. A couple of years later the New Romantics also embraced a style which broke down the barriers between private and public attire. But it was pop musicians, groups like Siouxsie and the Banshees, Soft Cell, and Frankie Goes to Hollywood, who were the most visible exponents of this tendency and who brought fetishistic iconography to a mass audience. It was in this climate – with fashion poised to embrace the pervy – that the invitations to Skin Two went out, and from the opening night it was clear that the dominating atmosphere would be one of trendy kinkiness.

Without the presence of glamorous youth and the odd pop star Skin Two's eventual impact would have been limited, but it wasn't the trendy, fashion-oriented kids on their own who made the evening seminal. The other component of the formula was the rich heritage that the 'serious' fetishists brought with them; for unlike the Sexual Revolution of the sixties, the Fetish Scene that Skin Two heralded has always possessed a past of which it is proud.

For example, amongst those present on the opening night of Skin Two was a man called John Sutcliffe, who back in the sixties had started up a little company called Atomage which made extraordinary leather catsuits and other bizarre outfits, some of which had been used in the stage play of *The Avengers* and almost all of which had cropped up in specialist fetish magazines like *Rubber Girls*. Little did Sutcliffe realize it, but the design aesthetic pioneered in these garments was ripe for interpretation by high fashion.

Also present on the opening night were a large number of devotees of the cult films of Betty Page, an American actress who had stylishly pranced her way through numerous short films in the fifties and sixties. While cheaply made, these little films had a lot of charm and, like the Atomage designs, they provided a visual clue to a brand of eroticism which aroused as much by what it concealed as by what it revealed.

Skin Two's 'serious fetishists' also brought with them a literary tradition which contained within it the makings of a philosophical base substantial enough to challenge the still-pervasive thesis of sexual casualness. There were those who could quote verbatim from de Sade's *Justine*, Georges Bataille's *The Story of the Eye* and Leopold von Sacher-Masoch's *Venus In Furs*. Far overshadowing all of these, however, was familiarity with Pauline Reage's extraordinary novel *The Story of O*.

The Story of O describes one woman's journey through various stages of erotic discovery. The catalogue of her humiliations and tortures is extensive and extreme but what sets *O* apart and ensured its importance with the Skin Two crowd was O's complicity in her humiliations and tortures. While de Sade's (or even Bataille's) victims simply encounter their fate as one might be run over by a number 28 bus, O possesses volition – choosing (or at least not choosing to flee from) her subjugation and degradation.

This is an important distinction because it underlines the way in which those at Skin Two saw their own sexual/erotic adventures as a journey of self-discovery. O – naked, whipped, abused, demeaned – loses all human dignity but simultaneously acquires a new, sublime dignity. By eschewing easy pleasures, by accommodating indignity and pain, O opens the door of erotic and existential possibility.

If O's journey provided a logical (even a spiritual) rationale for the Skin Two experiment, Reage's attention to stylish detail also defined an aesthetic sensibility which had enormous appeal. Unlike a character from de Sade – and most certainly unlike any character in a porn film – O was *chic*.

It was this that would mark Skin Two's most immediate impact beyond the confines of this little club in Soho as Daniel James, Ectomorph, Kim West, Fetish Or Die and a host of other designers found ways of translating the imagery of erotic obsession into provocative – but always stylish – fashion. And when the sleek gloss of these garments was photographed by the likes of Bob Carlos Clarke, Peter Ashworth, Kevin Davis and Trevor Watson, a point was reached where previously ghettoized obsessions became part of the fabric of mainstream culture.

Meanwhile from one club came many: Maitress, Der Putsch, Madame Venus, Submission, Severin's Kiss, Fantastic!, Torture Garden, Valkyrie, Whiplash, Tears of Eros, Demask (Amsterdam); Club Caprice (Stuttgart); Doma (Den Haag); Treff Bazarr (Düsseldorf); Highlights (Munich); Hjarter Dam (Stockholm); Fetish Factor, the Vault, House of Domination, Paddles, Jackie 60,

Tattooed Love Child (New York); Fetish (Miami); Sin-A-Matic (LA); the Hellfire Club (Melbourne, Sydney and Brisbane); Discipline Gym and The Deep (Tokyo).

Magazines and videos also proliferated: *Skin Two* (the magazine), *O* (German and English editions), *Ritual*, *Zeitgeist*, *Dèmonia* (France), *Secret* (Belgium), *A Taste of Latex*, *Venus in Furs* (USA), X-Ulmanen (from Finland, in English).

And now a new generation of 'fetish fashion' designers like Murray & Vern, Libidex, Wild Designs, Julian Latorre, Loco, Modern Armour, Pagan Metal, Demask and Jack the Rubber can take for granted that their creations may crop up in the pages of *Vogue* or provide inspiration for the highest of high fashion throughout the world.

When Skin Two was opened back in 1983 we all sensed that something interesting was happening, but I'm sure that none of us gathered in that grotty little venue hidden up an alley in London's Soho imagined the potential of this blend of slick trendiness and serious perversity. At the time we had all seen far too many cults come and go to consider longevity to be very likely. But now, more than ten years on, Skin Two has grown into a huge international empire with a magazine, a shop, a mail order outlet, a publications division and periodic party events which attract partygoers in their thousands. Clearly this is not a passing fad.

Neither is it just a fashion. Beyond the style there is substance – a lifestyle, an ideology, a vision of how people might ideally relate to one another sexually.

One of the earliest Fetish Scene clubs after Skin Two called itself Der Putsch, which is German for an uprising or revolution. At the time many of us thought this an odd name for a club where you could do your thing in your new rubber outfit from Daniel James or Ectomorph. But, in retrospect, it's clear that the name was appropriate and prophetic: this isn't just a fancy dress party, it's a revolution; a second Sexual Revolution which marks a radical break with its sixties' predecessor and which promotes a complete, top-to-bottom reappraisal of the nature of liberation. Whether this revolution can deliver all that it promises remains to be seen. In my lifetime I've witnessed and believed in another sexual revolution and I'm therefore inclined to a certain degree of cynicism. But what does seem beyond doubt is the fact that the Scene's vision of a sexuality beyond casual encounter – beyond, in other words, the flippancy of pop sex – holds great appeal for an ever-growing number of people.

'Post-modernism' is one of the most overused and irritating terms in our vocabulary. It gained prominence in the eighties as a description of a style of architecture that thumbed its nose at the 'modern' styles of the sixties – by daring to incorporate decoration for its own sake, a backward glance at history and a sense of humour – and then became tiresomely obligatory in describing developments in everything from furniture to food, pop music to philosophy. Despite this, I'm going to propose it as an appropriate label for the approach to sexuality which has evolved within the Fetish Scene.

It is an appropriate term first because it reminds us that sexuality is always embedded in and reflects the world around it. For sexuality *not* to be a cliché it would have to be defined by genetics rather than by culture (something which is true of all creatures except ourselves). If we live in a post-modern age it is inevitable that our sexuality should acquire the same characteristics.

Second, 'post-modern sex' is an appropriate label because the sexual system from which it evolved, but from which it now seeks to set itself apart, defined itself as 'modern'. We can see this clearly in Michael Leigh's account of the early days of the sixties' sexual revolution, *The Velvet Underground*. Almost without exception the swingers' personal ads which appeared in newspapers and magazines throughout America (and which Leigh reproduces) employ the phrases 'modern couple', 'modern relationship', 'modern party' and 'modern sex'.

Leigh's subjects never actually get round to spelling out what exactly they mean by this usage but its meaning is clear: 'modern sex' is uninhibited, has no patience with old-fashioned coyness, hesitancy and ritual, gets down to the nitty-gritty without delay. In short, therefore, modern sex, like modern design, is *functional*.

In contrast, *post*-modern sexuality, like post-modern design, takes functionalism with a pinch of salt. (Or, to be more precise, it recognizes a broader definition of 'functional' so as to incorporate that which is not generally seen as 'practical' but which of course is just that.) If the modern sex of Michael Leigh's swingers (and their descendants doing their thing in Plato's Retreat) saw its objective as drawing the shortest possible line between arousal and release, the post-modern sex of the Scene delights in placing impediments in the path of this 'functional' and 'practical' imperative. These impediments take the form of complex rituals, a substitution of fetish for the naked body as the immediate object of desire, the re-routing of pleasure into pain, and the hesitancy entailed in bondage and the dominant's discipline and control. Like a post-modern chair that seems to have been designed as a piece of sculpture rather than something to sit on, post-modern sex deliberately turns its back on the comfort of immediate sexual release.

It is this refusal to accept too narrow and simplistic a definition of 'function' (an uncomfortable chair may serve other purposes; sexual experience may have other objectives than the release of pent-up libido) which most pointedly identifies the linkage between Scene sex and post-modern design. But there are other similarities: both respect history – looking backward in order to look forward, mocking the sixties' idea that the future must be 'liberated' from the past. Both dwell in a world of symbolism – endeavouring to be thought-provoking, conceptual as well as sensual. Both are unrepentantly eclectic – sampling from sources as diverse as possible, refusing to accept traditional distinctions between 'good' and 'bad' taste, high and low culture. Getting off on the mix. Both recognize the value of imagination and fantasy – rejecting the modern notion that reason and logic alone are sufficient. And both, at their best, enjoy a sense of humour.

Just as post-modern design arose and prospered as an antidote to the sterility of (bad) modernism, so Post-modern sex must be seen as a way out of Café Flesh. Had 'modern sex', as proposed by the swingers, the playboys or the hippies, delivered what it promised, the Scene would never have prospered and would never have insinuated itself into our culture's constructs of desire.

Post-modern, Scene sex responds to all the facets of our contemporary world's sexual crises: to the withering of seduction and erotic nuance within the desert of instant gratification, it responds, 'What's the rush?' And, 'Is not the pleasure in the journey rather than the arrival?' To feminism's tussle with the question of how sex and power can function within a heterosexual context, it responds: 'In sexual matters someone is always going to be on top, but why presume any inherent link between "topness" and gender?' To those uncertain about gender identity in a world where 'male' and 'female' roles are increasingly problematic, it responds: 'What does it matter what genital equipment you happen to have been born with? Why not invent a brand new gender for yourself?' To the dark shadow of AIDS, it responds: 'What's so special about penetrative sex?' And, 'Why screw around when you can better explore infinite erotic possibility within a stable relationship?'

This last point is important, for while I have argued throughout this chapter that the sixties' Sexual Revolution was doomed from the start by its own naïvety, AIDS has in a sense rendered the whole issue academic. Even if pop sex had succeeded it would have failed in the context of Death By Sex. Like it or not, casual sex, the bottom line of sixties-style liberation, is no longer a viable option. Like it or not, today's key question is, 'How can sexual excitement be kept alive within a long-term, stable relationship?' And, like it or not, it is the sexual strategy of the Fetish and S/M Scene which seems best placed to answer this question.

'Hot Monogamy' is a phrase coined by Dr Helen Singer Kaplan of the New York Hospital Cornell Center's Human Sexuality Program. While there are undoubtedly ways of increasing the temperature of monogamy which aesthetically and ideologically are far removed from Scene sex, the fact remains that it is within this particular erotic laboratory that experimentation on this problem is most advanced.

What hundreds, even thousands of couples like those photographed and interviewed in this book have discovered is that monogamy can successfully be kept at boiling point by means of such practices as role-playing power games where Sub/Dom divisions are rendered explicit, by making an exhibition of yourself and/or your partner, by watching and getting off on the games that others play, by controlling the pace of lust's impatience by means of symbolic ritual and actual restraint, by using pain to intensify or highlight pleasure and by simply allowing fantasy and the imagination to flourish in the mind's eye.

Many will object that these are dangerous practices which should be avoided. I am aware of the dangers and will consider them in the final chapter, but is not AIDS a greater and more immediate danger? And if they found a cure for AIDS tomorrow, what of the dangers of Café Flesh where the *frisson* of desire and seduction have been annihilated and where all that remains is the virus of insatiable titillation? Drastic situations require drastic solutions.

CARL/ANNIE

HOUSK   What is it about S/M that interests you?

ANNIE   Well . . . since I was really young I've had this in my head. I used to have wet dreams based on S/M fantasies when I was eight, and I've always figured one day it would become reality.

HOUSK   How about you, Carl; is this something you've always wanted?

No, and I don't think it will become central to our sex lives, it's just a fun **CARL**
addition.

What is it about bondage that attracts you? HOUSK

Being restricted, a touch of danger. But since you're with someone you **CARL**
trust you know there's no danger really. See, I might be kissing Annie
and want my hands bound so I can't touch her, but for that to work she'd
have to feel my need and just do it. It would spoil it if I had to ask.

ANNIE	I like to be held down firmly too . . . but gently.
HOUSK	So you're not into being hurt?
ANNIE	Oh no, I don't think I like real pain, though I wish Carl would sometimes hurt me more than he does; but nothing excruciating. You see, Carl and I are just beginning to discover this side of us, we're both new to it and that's nice, we can can find our own pace. I also like spanking . . . you know, being spanked.
HOUSK	When did you realize this?
ANNIE	I think I've always known it. Not just being spanked on my bottom but being roughed up, too — not in a horrible way, though, just a big man being powerful with me. God knows where that comes from! My sister feels the same.
HOUSK	How rough do you mean — bruised?
ANNIE	I don't know. If I got excited enough there's no saying where my cut-off point would be. Luckily Carl has more control than me, so I'm safe.
CARL	I wouldn't force anyone into anything.
ANNIE	But what if I wanted it?
CARL	Annie, I'm so much stronger than you. This is just a fantasy of yours, you wouldn't like it if I really hurt you.

Well, I don't know . . . maybe I would.

Oh, come on, if I pinned you against a wall and forced you to do
whatever I wanted, you wouldn't like it.

ANNIE

CARL

ANNIE	You're probably right. I'd want it done my way.
HOUSK	Carl, does spanking do anything for you?
CARL	Yes, it gives me a naughty, sort of elfin buzz.
ANNIE	Doesn't it excite you? Don't you get a big hard-on? For me it's really sexual, makes me want to get fucked.
CARL	Well, if I feel you getting wet then I get turned on but the spanking alone doesn't do much for me.

ANNIE

I also like the schoolgirl thing, being really young and about to be punished for doing something bad. Sometimes I like to make love to Carl like he's a woman and I pretend I'm a man because, even though he's big,

> **Sometimes I like to make love to Carl like he's a woman and I pretend I'm a man**

he's very gentle. But I think this is more my fantasy than his.

HOUSK

Do either of you have any fetishes?

CARL

Yes, definitely. I love leather. Before I met Annie, if I went to a club I'd sometimes come home and leave my leathers on when I went to bed because I love the smell so much; just the feel of it turns me on.

ANNIE

For me it's tight lingerie, nothing loose or baggy. I often wear it during sex because it makes me feel hornier.

HOUSK

So what do you hope to get from sex?

ANNIE

Oh, a closeness. It's an expression of our love for each other but our relationship is not based on it by a long way.

CARL

We try to mingle together, become one. It's like there are times we feel we just can't get close enough.

FETISHISM

In the mid-fifteenth century Portuguese explorers in pursuit of a route to Asia worked their way down the west coast of Africa. How wide their eyes must have been, how confused their thoughts, as they first came into contact with ways of life untouched by Europe – an experience which today could only be matched by the arrival of extraterrestrials. So many things must have amazed them, but the one which history has focused upon is their fascination with the way the tribal peoples of West Africa believed that certain seemingly unmiraculous objects – a stone, a knotted string, an animal pelt, an amulet – possessed magical powers. The Portuguese used the word *feitico* to describe these tribal objects, meaning 'charming', and deriving from the Latin *carmen*, which literally means 'song' but also denotes the power which music can possess.

While today we may have stripped the word charm of most of its original significance, to the fifteenth-century Portuguese it was no trifling adjective. These explorers knew full well how a siren song, a beautiful woman or the devil himself might captivate the soul and they would have afforded the charming a potency which today we tend to ignore.

It is in this sense that we should understand the explorers' use of the word *feitico*, and, therefore, its descendant term 'fetish'. For though Europe has had its spiritually powerful, charmed objects – supposed fragments of Christ's shroud or body and of course the cross – it would take many centuries before the exclusively 'primitive' associations of enchanted objects might be questioned; centuries, that is, before it would occur to the West that we too might be fetishists.

It was perhaps Karl Marx who most imaginatively injected the notion of fetishism into a Western context when he sought to describe the 'double alienation' of industrialized society, whereby human relations become objectified while at the same time objects acquire human-like 'value' above their station. Thus, in Marx's view, a 'trivial thing' like a table becomes 'a very queer thing, abounding in metaphysical subtleties'. This shift from matter-of-fact utility to something which seems to possess a will of its own (something of 'value' and seductive power) Marx termed 'commodity fetishism'.[1]

Although there are clearly links which might be made between this 'secret', persuasive power of objects and sexual desire, as far as I am aware Marx did not elaborate them. It is, of course, Sigmund Freud whose name is most closely associated with the transposition of fetishism into the sphere of sexuality. It is a mistake, however, to presume that Freud invented this usage. Richard von Krafft-Ebing's *Psychopathia Sexualis* (1886) lists 'fetishism' amongst the more important sexual 'perversions', attributing it to something he called 'heredito-degenerescence'. Unhappy with this assumption that sexual fetishism is some-how genetically induced, Alfred Binet (better known as the inventor of the intelligence test) published his essay 'Le fétichisme dans l'amour' the following year, in 1887.

Emily Apter, in her fascinating book *Feminizing the Fetish: Psychoanalysis and Narrative Obsession in Turn-of-the-Century France*, sees this essay by Binet as seminal, the first significant attempt to place sexual fetishism within the domain of psychology. For Binet:

The term *fetishism*, it seems to us, is rather appropriate for this genre of sexual perversion. The adoration these patients exhibit toward inert objects such as the nightcap or the bootnail resembles on every level the adoration exhibited by the savage or Negro toward fish-bones or shiny pebbles, with this single important difference that, in the cult of our patients, religious adoration is replaced by sexual appetite.[2]

What makes Binet's essay significant is his presumption that such perverse 'erotic rumination' is triggered in the individual not by some innate inheritance, but rather by some traumatic incident in that individual's life. Where Freud takes over from Binet is in spelling out exactly what kind of traumatic incident might have this effect – namely, the sight of a naked female. The trauma, according to Freud, lies in the fact that females lack a penis (a notion which, especially to the reader unfamiliar with Freud's theory of fetishism, might itself be a bit traumatic). But, however bizarre, given that this idea has become the foundation of psychoanalytical thinking on the subject of fetishism, it is important to give Freud's theory a hearing:

> This abnormality [fetishism], which may be counted as one of the perversions, is, as is well known, based on the patient (who is almost always male) not recognizing the fact that females have no penis – a fact which is extremely undesirable to him since it is a proof of the possibility of his being castrated himself. He therefore disavows his own sense-perception which showed him that the female genitals lack a penis and holds fast to the contrary conviction. The disavowed perception does not, however, remain entirely without influence for, in spite of everything, he has not the courage to assert that he actually saw a penis. He takes hold of something else instead – a part of the body or some other object – and assigns it the role of the penis which he cannot do without. It is usually something that he in fact saw at the moment at which he saw the female genitals, or it is something that can suitably serve as a symbolic substitute for the penis.[3]

In this way, not only does Freud (like Binet) reclassify the fetishist as 'patient' but he also manages to drain the concept of fetishism of any enchantment.

Instead of a 'magic object' the fetish is reduced to the status of pathetic substitute, a 'joke' penis, a mistake. It is Freud's clinical tone as much as his theory which accomplishes this: giving not the slightest acknowledgement that that which is 'charming' might warrant some respect, his language is that of a repair manual of pathology.

And what exactly is it that needs fixing? In his 'Three Essays on the Theory of Sexuality' Freud makes this all too clear: 'Perversions are sexual activities which either (a) extend, in an anatomical sense, beyond the regions of the body that are designed for sexual union, or (b) linger over the intermediate relations to the sexual object which should normally be traversed rapidly on the path towards the final sexual aim'.[4] The fetishist – guilty on both counts – must be cured of this perverse 'lingering'.

All of which would at least be amusing if someone other than Freud – someone who wasn't a mechanic, someone with respect for the magical, Jung perhaps – had had his ideas become the primary component of modern sexual theory. Or, perhaps, *her* theories – for, when all is said and done, is not the crux of the problem located in Freud's crotch?

DEBBIE/JENI

Does either of you have a fetish for any particular material?	HOUSK
Rubber and silk.	**DEBBIE**
Yeah, velvet silk . . . ohh!	**JENI**
I've got this dress my mother gave to me that's been made of specially	**DEBBIE**

dipped rubber that never needs to be polished and it's so soft it feels like silk, so I get both sensations . . . it's brilliant. I've had so many pleasurable experiences involving rubber that its smell alone sets off exciting memories.

JENI   I feel the same, though I'm also turned on by the smell of leather. When I wear rubber it's the sweating that gets me horny, feeling my skin sliding underneath is great . . . I can get off on myself.

DEBBIE   Wearing loose rubber is special too. It causes static so you can feel all your hairs stand up. That, plus the swishing sound it makes when you move, is wonderful. There are times when I'm sitting down in my shop, Libido, and I'm just listening to customers trying on rubber outfits when all of a sudden I'll get empathy chills and goosebumps of excitement. The smell of rubber is nice, too. If I've been dancing for a while I'll pull open the front of my dress and stick my head inside and get this rush of rubbery sweat and sex . . . it's wonderful, you could bottle and sell it.

HOUSK   When did you first get involved with the Scene?

DEBBIE   S/M and sex came together for me round about the same time . . . when I was seventeen. I'd wanked and played around before but I'm talking

about intercourse. I lost my virginity and discovered S/M all at once. It's
something I feel very comfortable with, though there are times I don't
want to do it. I guess you could say S/M's something I like, but I'm not

obsessed with it. I wouldn't want that to happen because then it would lose the fun element.

JENI   S/M's been on my mind since I was fifteen because I knew people who were into it. I haven't actually done much up until now, though I've wanted to. It's hard to find the right person. You see, I really like the idea of being submissive but I've always been afraid to ask — I thought no one would take me seriously because I'm so young. Oh, I've managed to get a few guys to dominate me but never women, and they're my main passion. That is, of course, until Debbie. Most women want me to be dominant because I seem so confident but I'm not really, so it doesn't work. S/M is more a desire than a regular reality for me and I'm really not into the pain so much as being submissive.

HOUSK   Will you accept pain in order to be dominated?

JENI   Yeah.

HOUSK   Do either of you have any special interests?

DEBBIE   Yes, I have an absolute fascination with surgeons' rubber gloves and internal examinations, speculums, etc. It's so vulnerable. I like being examined and being the examiner. It's a trust thing but I need the rubber gloves. The sound of them going on and the snap as you get them over your wrists tells me this is serious, the real business.

I have an absolute fascination with surgeons' rubber gloves and internal examinations

JENI   Yes, it's the vulnerability thing, not knowing what's coming next but trusting the other person anyway. Though part of my thrill is imagining that the other person has snapped and I'm tied and helpless.

DEBBIE   I also have a fetish for surgical equipment: all that gleaming stainless steel . . . so cold . . . the clinking sound of metal, it's all important. In

bondage I like the sound of flesh straining against leather rather than rope. Also, if you're punishing with a cane, the swish through the air behind a blindfolded partner is a large part of the thrill, the anticipation. You watch to see if they flinch and then build up the tension as they wait for the hurt.

That's so true. If I'm blindfolded I like to hear the rustle of bags, because **JENI** I don't know what's coming out of them to be used on me. I remember

once I was sure Debbie was going to use the speculum because of all the clinking and clanking, but it was a strap-on instead and since I'd been prepared for cold metal it was a real surprise! Good, though.

DEBBIE I'd hidden everything from Jeni beforehand so she had no idea what I was up to. You see, what really helps is that I've tried everything first myself before I do it to someone else, so I'm able to share the experience with them fully.

Do you find S/M satisfying outside of a relationship?

If I'm working, dominating another person, it's a different thing. I don't get sexually aroused, I get on a power trip instead, people putting themselves at my mercy, so to speak. I'm turning them on, I'm in control. When I'm with my partner it's different, there's love.

I love ladies' knickers (I mean real ones, not boring briefs), their shape, silkiness and elastics thrill me to the point of ejaculation, which I confess often happens. I get much enjoyment from photos of ladies showing their knickers and young Maureen J. D.'s rounded knickered bottom beautifully displayed in *Relate* no. 9 brought me much pleasure. In fact it prompted me to some further purchases of directoire knickers [knickers with long, elasticated legs which were fashionable earlier this century].

In my town we are fortunate in having an old-fashioned draper's run by a kindly middle-aged lady. In two or three years I must have bought upwards of 2 dozen pairs of knickers (and other delectable things) from her. Having seen Maureen's photos I could not resist talking to someone about knickers so I phoned my undie shop and asked on the phone for a couple of pairs of pink directoire knickers to be put aside. My lady in the shop replied by asking if I was the gentleman who often comes in, 'if so, I will willingly do this for you'. I shortly afterwards called in and as she spread the exquisite things over the counter she told me they were becoming difficult for her to get . . .

Yours,

'Knickerbockerglory'

This letter appeared in *Relate: An Illustrated Journal of Correspondence*,[5] a magazine which no longer seems to exist but which in the seventies allowed 'enthusiasts' of all persuasions a chance to share what had previously been the loneliest of secrets. There were some, like 'Knickerbockerglory', for whom only baggy directoire knickers would do but there were also those whose 'thing' was stilettos, or corsets, Wellington boots, nurses' uniforms, stockings and suspenders, French maid outfits, gas masks, leather, PVC or rubber. (And for the last group of enthusiasts a regular 'Rubber Wife of the Month' feature.)

Like Knickerbockerglory's letter, most of the correspondence in *Relate* seemed to fit neatly into Freud's model of fetishism: from an early age some particular garment, material or part of the human body is invested with extraordinary erotic power such that sexual satisfaction – or even arousal – cannot occur without the presence of the particular fetish object. Also, although *Relate* featured photographs of wives and girlfriends wearing all manner of apparel, they were typically presented as fetishized rather than fetishists: the unavoidable impression was that the 'real fetishists' were men.

This last point is of course crucial to Freud and his followers because if, as they argue, the fetishistic focus is motivated by fear of losing one's penis, then it follows that one must possess such an appendage in order to worry about losing it. As we saw in the previous section, Freud himself wrote that the fetishist is 'almost always male'. But why the 'almost' which surely in its hesitancy threatens the entire theory? To make matters worse (but much more interesting) we learn from Emily Apter's *Feminizing the Fetish* that some previously unpublished minutes of the Vienna Psychoanalytic Society have Freud on record as stating categorically, and in complete contradiction to his other writings, that 'half of humanity must be classed among the clothes fetishists. All women, that is, are clothes fetishists. Dress plays a puzzling role in them.'[6]

To have any hope of making sense of this crucial issue we need to approach it from a different perspective. In 1930 J. C. Flugel published a book entitled *The Psychology of Clothes* in which he, amongst other things, considered what he termed 'The Great Masculine Renunciation', namely:

The sudden reduction of male sartorial decorativeness which took place at the end of the eighteenth century. At about that time there occurred one of the most remarkable events in the whole history of dress, one under the influence of which we are still living, one, moreover, which has attracted far less attention than it deserves: men gave up their right to all the brighter, gayer, more elaborate, and more varied forms of ornamentation, leaving these entirely to the use of women . . . Man abandoned his claim to be considered beautiful. He henceforth aimed at being only useful.[7]

Flugel, a psychologist, was of the view that this renunciation had triggered worrying psychological problems which festered under the surface. Aside from transvestism, Flugel does not spell out these problems specifically but it seems to me that fetishism (and also Freud's theory of fetishism) could be considered profitably in this context.

The effect of the Great Masculine Renunciation was to leave men without bodies – strange, robotically 'useful' creatures equipped only with brains and penises. Freud himself was, of course, a perfect example of post-Renunciation man and can it be any wonder therefore that he and his male contemporaries were so obsessed with male genitals? For this appendage was all that remained of their corporal reality, their only instrument of expressing themselves physically. That this was also clearly true of Freud's male patients in some ways underlines a validity inherent in his theory of fetishism: with the male body compressed into the penis, its loss could not be contemplated and a second – spare – penis would have to be found in the form of the fetish.

And the consequences of the Great Masculine Renunciation can be pursued even further. Aside from stripping men of their joy in flamboyantly decorating their bodies, it also left them perilously exposed to *categorization* as 'fetishists'. What might previously have been seen as 'love of fashion' would, post-Renunciation, be labelled 'pathological'. In this way it could be said that the Great Masculine Renunciation *created* fetishism as perversion.

Here's a thought: if we were to allow 'All women are fetishists' as a correct statement but, instead of mocking this condition as Freud did, we broadened it to the view that at heart all men are fetishists as well, we would remove the stigma attached to what Freud called 'the demands of fashion' – for surely to label something typical of all of humanity as pathological is itself perverse?

The fetishistic, charming powers of dress and adornment – including their erotic puissance – have always existed. Such powers, however, are not inherently pathological: it was only when nineteenth-century man attempted to disassociate himself from them that he ironically, and sadly, rendered them perversely potent. The core of the problem is that with the advent of the Great Masculine Renunciation the fetishistic, charming power of apparel came to reside only in 'women's things'. This is important, first, because (for the heterosexual male) fetishistic power was monopolized by the erotic. And second, because – except for the transvestite – this power could no longer be embraced directly, personally by men.

One effect of all this was to convert women into surrogate bodies so that, through them, men might still participate in the pleasure of dress and attire. In the process, women were objectified as 'clothes hangers' – the person–object relationship which men had come to deny themselves now transposed to male–female relations.

The other effect was upon men themselves, as fetishistic obsession – focused in upon itself – festered in the masculine psyche.

The problem is not that objects possess power. The problem arises when there is an excessive focusing and short-circuiting of this power brought about by a perverse estrangement from the generalized power of dress and adornment.

Here are Freud's patients in Vienna with their sexuality, their relations, their souls compressed into tiny relics of desire – a glove, a lock of hair, a shoe. Their desire is as much for an absent physicality as for some mythic sexual Other. Here too is Freud himself, striving to take away the glove, the lock of hair and the shoe but offering nothing magical or potent in its place.

But it is a long time since the Great Masculine Renunciation decreed that a Real Man can find no delight in his own apparel and appearance, and this presumption no longer passes unchallenged. Within my lifetime the 'unisex' tendencies of the sixties have blossomed into the 'gender bending' of Glam, Punk, New Romantics and Rave, with the result that – while we still have a long way to go – even a Joe Normal can experiment with his appearance in ways hitherto denied post-Renunciation man. Is this why the accounts of Freud's famous patients and the letters of the likes of 'Knickerbockerglory' seem so distant from contemporary experience?

The age of fetishism is certainly not over and done with – far from it – but that particular kind of stereotypical male fetishist seems less common today. Rather than craving a spare penis, such classical fetishists were desperately seeking a body to dress up, show off and delight in. If this particular genre of fetishism is on the decline it is because the Great Masculine Renunciation has itself, to an extent, been renounced. This is a matter of culture rather than biology and it is of course precisely this which Freud and his colleagues failed to take into account. Realizing that something very odd was going on with his male patients, Freud looked to their genitals when he should have looked to the excessively restricting and downright peculiar definition of 'masculinity' within which they (and he) found themselves.

The result was a smokescreen which for too long has obscured the straightforwardness of the process whereby objects become synonyms of desire.

Near the start of Marcel Proust's epic novel *Remembrance of Things Past* the protagonist, Swann, happens to eat a certain kind of biscuit – a 'petite madeleine' – and its distinctive taste triggers a flood of memories which continues through seven volumes. In real life our memories may not achieve such complexity but the process is exactly the same: a taste, a smell, a colour, a tactile sensation unlocks a remembrance of things past. We may be unaware of what is going on consciously, but nevertheless our lives are an infinitely layered construction of connections between objects and the memories with which they have become associated.

Of course many of these associations are erotic in character and the objects which trigger them – objects which might or might not be traditionally categorized as 'sexy' – are thereby drawn into the sexual domain. If you have a memorable sexual experience while lying on lavender-coloured sheets, from this point on the colour lavender will contain within its various associations a sexual component. This simple, universal process is, it seems to me, the bottom line of fetishism.

Accordingly, *any* object (or physical quality) can be fetishistic. The erotic power is not necessarily inherent in the nature of the object: if a sexual association develops, it does so by happenstance and for this reason that which pushes a button marked 'arousal' for person A may seem completely without sexual connotation for persons B, C and D.

Such fetishes are personal and idiosyncratic but there are also objects that acquire wider status as 'fetish objects'. Garments made of rubber are a good example of this. When first made and mass produced around the time of the First World War, such garments were seen as utilitarian rather than fetishistic. It was only several decades later that this new and practical material became synonymous with kinkiness. In the interim period I'm sure that many individuals experienced situations that triggered an association between rubber clothing and sexual excitement but it took time for the rubber=kinky/sexy connotation to become institutionalized. At first this new association was accepted only by a minority group of 'enthusiasts', but by the late eighties the whole of Western culture – taking its cue from high fashion – agreed to categorize rubber, together with leather, PVC, satin and silk, as 'sexy'.

Whether the transition from personal to cultural fetish occurs because of chance or some quality inherent in an object/material is hard to say. To continue with the example of latex garments, one could surmise that latex made this transition simply because it was associated with having sex out of doors (rubber capes and macs were once popular for country strolls; they also served as protection from damp grass), but then again, any rubber enthusiast will extol the *inherent* sexy qualities of this material: the way that rubber amplifies touch, clings to the body, generates *frisson* in its rapid transition from hot to cold.

Obviously once a fetish object has been widely accepted as such, its sexual power will become a self-fulfilling prophecy. This occurs first because henceforth the object/material will typically be photographically portrayed in a visual style which is itself erotically charged. And second because such mass exposure means that more and more people are likely to encounter the fetish object/material and henceforth include it in their own personal set of erotic associations. (Or to put this another way: we accumulate our personal repertoire of fetishistic objects both from unique, 'real life' experiences and also from impressions that flood into our lives second-hand, via the media.)

So far I have avoided placing fetishism within a context of pathology; that the colour lavender, latex garments or, say, the scent of Poison perfume might have sexually positive associations is surely not problematic. It might become so, however, if *only* lavender, latex or Poison possessed such power for a given individual. It is, in other words, not fetishistic power *per se* but rather the *range* of a person's fetishistic repertoire that may or may not define fetishism as a 'problem'.

For most people a variety of sexual experiences generates a wide range of erotic object associations. Lavender sheets are followed by white ones, pink ones, floral printed ones. Unfortunate circumstances may, however, limit this range at a critical point in an individual's life and then presumably an unhealthy focusing might follow. For example, let's say that just prior to the outbreak of the Second World War a young man in Britain had his first sexual experience with a woman while lying on a rubber mac in a meadow. While previously our young man might only have associated rubber mackintoshes with practicality or fashion, now they have also acquired erotic associations. This is not in itself a problem. But if, say, he is then called up to military service and it is two long years before another sexual opportunity presents itself, one would not be surprised to discover that over the course of those years rubber macs have come to monopolize all erotic associations – eventually, perhaps, defining any sexual experience not involving rubber macs as unarousing.

This example also serves to introduce another interesting characteristic of fetishism: the way in which it is inevitably a museum of fashion. As is intrinsic in its nature, fashion is forever changing but although we may accumulate erotic object associations throughout our lives, there does seem to be a critical period (adolescence, or perhaps earlier) when the most potent links between objects and arousal become fixed in our minds. Fashion moves on from this point in time but erotically we tend to remain time-warped in the era of our youth, with the result that those garments or materials which provoke our desires come to seem increasingly odd, bizarre, perverse and 'fetishistic' to other, younger eyes.

Take the example of the corset. In his awesomely comprehensive book *Fashion and Fetishism* David Kunzle traces the long history of this garment into and out of fashion – at the same time showing how even during its unfashionable periods, a minority 'fetishistic' fascination remained. (The quotation marks are there because the erotic power has existed all along: it was only *defined* as 'fetishistic' once the 'fashion'. label had been removed.) Today there is a group in Britain which gathers regularly for the purpose of celebrating the corset and 'tight lacing'. One can't help but notice how many of this group are of 'a certain age' which, when you work it out, is precisely the generation that entered adolescence around the time when the corseted 'wasp waist' of Dior's 'New Look' was all the rage.

What, one wonders, will be the fetishistic obsession of today's youth twenty or thirty years from now? The answer, I suspect, is everything and so, in a sense, nothing – for contemporary fashion has lost its totalitarian singularity and, in a way that is without historical precedent, has embraced extreme stylistic pluralism. These days fashions from the forties, fifties, sixties and seventies are continually recycled while at the same time the members of various 'styletribes' remain faithful year in and year out to certain 'classics'. All this jumbled together cheek by jowl creates an extraordinary supermarket of style from which we pick and mix a personal style. And a fetishistic repertoire.

This picking and mixing is a different process from the acquisition of a fetish object through happenstance and, unlike the latter process, it underlines the symbolic, meaningful characteristics of such objects. Rubber, leather, PVC, satin, silk, fur, corsets, G-strings, stilettos, masks, nurses' uniforms, *et al*, each has something specific to 'say'. While in the classic fetish scenario of acquisition by chance the message of object/material X, Y or Z prescribes a given erotic vision, in the present day supermarket-of-style scenario an individual's particular erotic vision prescribes the selection of a certain set of objects/materials whose 'vocabulary' is symbolically suited to the expression of that vision.

Although it is undoubtedly true that every individual's erotic visions and dreams are unique, it is also true to say that these typically tend to fall within certain recognizable parameters: the Futuristic vs the Historic, the Beast vs the Sex Machine, the Aggressive/Dominant vs the Passive/Submissive, the Elitist vs the Egalitarian, the Controlled vs the Unrestrained, the Exotic vs the Domestic, the Enclosed vs the Open, etc. Whatever one's erotic profile, a suitable set and combination of object/material 'adjectives' can be found to articulate that profile. Thus a traditional, Victorian-style corset symbolically expresses the Historic, the Controlled and the Elite while a PVC catsuit proclaims the Futuristic, the Sex Machine and the Enclosed. Such terms are of course only crude approximations of such messages because words in general are so ill-suited to visionary expression – which is precisely why fetishistic objects are so important as tools of erotic realization.

The recent, extraordinary explosion of different 'fetish fashion' design companies (Britain's 'Catalogue Connection' mail-order company currently offers some forty-four different catalogues) coupled with our post-modern willingness to juxtapose different styles within one 'look' has created a very precise erotic language. At a club like Submission or the Torture Garden, where hundreds of different garment styles are to be seen, what takes the breath away is just how many different, unique 'statements' can be constructed from a handful of· fetishistic 'adjectives', each answering the question 'What is sex?' in a particular way, each pointing to some far-flung galaxy of erotic possibility.

But all convey one additional, shared message of fetishistic perviness. This is a message that, hitherto, our culture has sought to hide rather than proclaim from the roof tops. It remains for us to consider, therefore, why it should be that fetishism – historically fashion's embarrassing relation – has become its pride and joy.

It is one thing to consider why a particular individual might become fetishistically obsessed, quite another to consider why an entire culture might proceed down the same path.

Can there be any doubt about the extraordinary extent to which fetishism now flavours our aesthetic sensibilities and monopolizes our definition of the erotic?

In the pop music world, we've had Madonna in those famous conical bras and corsets, and number-one-charting rave group The Shamen performing on *Top of the Pops* dressed from head to toe in skin-tight, studded rubber, while even sweet Kylie Minogue has swapped her innocent *Neighbours* style for PVC basque and killer stilettos. In the cinema, Michelle Pfeiffer's gleaming latex catwoman catsuit prevented *Batman Returns* from sinking into obscurity. And opera stars like Lesley Garrett now do their thing in outfits which look like they belong in some kinky sci-fi bordello.

But it is on the catwalks that the fetishistic tendency has been at its most obtrusive and relentless, where practically every international designer has been finding some way of either hinting or shouting their pervy inclinations.

Materials like latex which previously high fashion wouldn't have touched with a bargepole are now commonplace in the most exclusive of collections. Skyscraper stilettos and platforms, corsets, sleek catsuits, exposed suspender belts, *femme fatale*-style long gloves, back-laced, bum revealing dresses, gauntlets and even dog collars are now as often found in the pages of *Vogue* or *Elle* as in the sort of mail order catalogues that used to hide discreetly in brown paper wrappers.

Vivienne Westwood's corsets and Jean-Paul Gaultier's dresses made only of thin, buckled straps can perhaps be dismissed as attention-seeking oddities, but when Karl Lagerfeld for Chanel comes up with traditional tweed suits edged in glossy black PVC you realize the extent to which fashion's language has come to rely on adjectives of perversity.

Meanwhile a whole new genre of designers – those whose entire *raison d'être* is fetish fashion – have found themselves increasingly taken seriously by a media and a fashion industry which only a few years ago would have dismissed them as tacky or weird. Today, if you are young and trendy you wear latex and PVC outfits by the likes of Murray & Vern, Kim West, Ectomorph, Libidex, Wild Design, Ellen Schippers, Schwarze Mode, Julian Latorre or Modern Armour. As Dominic Bradbury commented in the garment trade paper *Fashion Weekly*:

> From the bedroom and the backstreet to clubland and the high street, fetish-inspired fashion and second-skin styling have made a move into the mainstream and are set to stay there. Walk into Miss Selfridge or Top Shop, Stirling Cooper or Boy and you now find the sort of skin-hugging silhouettes in leather, leatherette and PVC that were once the preserve of the specialists – mostly sex shops – and the mail order companies. The taboos surrounding PVC and latex are fading away, as they once fell away from leather, in a new era of acceptability and teasing sensuality.[8]

There are many factors that might be cited to explain this metamorphosis of the fetishist's secret obsessions into acceptable fashion. First, there is the simple fact that fashion, in its never-ending quest for the new and different, must periodically dip into the clandestine and stigmatized just as it must search the Third World for 'ethnic' inspiration and recycle the fashions of previous eras. But fetishistic styles found their way into mainstream fashion in the late eighties; half a decade on, they are hardly new and different. In fact their appeal remains almost in *defiance* of fashion's pursuit of perpetual novelty.

Second, the fashion industry has become economically dependent upon selling non-clothing items like perfume. For *these* purposes arresting imagery takes precedence over wearability. Obviously fetishism offers an easy means of achieving this objective, but this doesn't answer the more difficult question: why does the perfume-buying public find fetishistic imagery so appealing and glamorous when in other eras it would have viewed it as tacky? Nor does it explain why, in a recession-hit fashion industry, those garments that continue to sell – be they at the haute couture or the high street level – are so often fetishistic in nature.

While it is often true that the machinery of fashion changes and the internal structures of the fashion industry frequently generate styles which bear little relationship to what is going on in the Real World, in this instance I feel that it is some fundamental imperative of the Real World that shapes stylistic trends. What might this be? What is going on in the world today that lures us into the once-derided wardrobe of the fetishist?

As I indicated in 'Hot Monogamy', there is the *fin de siècle* argument which suggests that it is simply the sighting on the horizon of the century's end which drives us into a depraved frenzy. While this seems a very neat idea, it is hard to comprehend the mechanisms that might bring it into effect. It's a bit like astrology – you're drawn to its offer of easy explanation, but you can never quite work out why the position of Mars should have any bearing on whether you get that promotion at the office.

If one is looking for a general theory to explain the industrial/post-industrial world's fetishistic obsessions, I would have thought that Marx's notion of 'double alienation' offers more than most. Could it be that just as communism has crumpled, capitalism has finally succumbed to eating itself? You will recall that Marx suggested that human relations would become ever more objectified while at the same time objects would acquire human-like value and power. The designer eighties certainly saw 'commodity fetishism' carried to a point where even everyday objects – the Tizio lamp, the Braun calculator, the Filofax – achieved deification. And it was also the decade that saw the rise of fetish fashion. From matt black to shiny black – if you're going to have a fetish why not go for the genuine article?

And the other side of 'double alienation' cannot be ignored. Was it not inevitable in a world constantly defined within the omnipresent language of advertising and marketing that human relations would be transformed into an interfacing of objects? While this is obviously a process which has been going on for some time we should, I think, bear in mind the enormous strides made in advertising and marketing in the eighties and the fact that these have changed our lives more than is generally realized. In particular, the perfecting of research groups in the eighties made it possible to reach the parts that had previously eluded advertisers, targeting lifestyles and jump-cutting between consumer values and private relationships as never before.

Consider a photograph I have in front of me from the most recent *Demask* fetish fashion catalogue. Two people, a man and a woman, are embracing. Their bodies are covered in a second skin of latex. Even their heads are completely covered in strangely shaped rubber masks, punctured only by tiny, invisible holes for breathing. The shiny, smooth perfection of the latex makes them resemble robots, androids, cybernauts . . . machines. Wouldn't Marx have seen in this imagery of sexualized machines/dehumanized relations an ultimate demonstration of 'double alienation'?

If, like me, you find Marx's theory persuasive and yet *Demask* imagery appeals to you, then you are in something of a quandary. Might there not be a less negative and bleak explanation of fetishism's increasing allure? I suggest that the second skin characteristics of so much of contemporary fetish fashion offers a more straightforward clue: we want to be sexual and yet we also feel the need of a protective, restraining barrier. On the most practical level it is hardly surprising that the spectre of AIDS has generated a need for a metaphor of all encompassing protection. And on a deeper psychological level, might not the symbolic attraction of such imagery reside in its promise of *emotional* protection?

But while such defensiveness seems a very real component of contemporary life, another, more positive factor also seems apparent. As we saw in 'Hot Monogamy', there is a growing tendency to reject instant gratification in favour of more leisurely, convoluted pursuits. Freud saw such lingering as the very definition of perversity but today I suspect that even the most conservative of sex therapists would disagree. Taking your time, engaging in foreplay, even as an end in itself, is increasingly viewed as healthy, good sex and it is precisely at this point that fetishism's lingering seems so laudable – the perfect antidote to the 'get 'em off, get it on' dead-end of the sixties' Sexual Revolution.

In other words, fetishism's contemporary appeal seems to stem directly from its tendency to impede instant gratification. It can do this literally by imposing an impenetrable second skin but it can also accomplish it by means of other, less obvious diversions: the sensual *frisson* of materials like rubber, PVC, leather, silk or satin. Exhibitionist display. Voyeuristic pleasure. Experimentation with personal identity. The visualization of erotic visions.

Fetishism says, 'Wait, there is more.' The 'lingering' upon which it is predicated may not have been to Freud's liking and the 'more' on offer may seem perilously close to Marx's vision of people as objects and objects as people, but its power – its magic – remains undeniable. For when all is said and done, our rubber-clad *Demask* couple are not so different from the masked West African shamans whose visage first brought the word fetishism into our vocabulary – disturbing, yes, but also charming, enchanted and miraculous.

ALAN/LOUIZA

Alan, you run one of the main fetish clubs in London. Are you personally involved in the Scene?

HOUSK

I know I do all these clubs and have the look but, for me, it's about having an interesting night out. I came up through the Goth Scene, a bit too late, so I missed the best clubs, which were about really dressing up and

ALAN

there were performances and visuals . . . a real sense of occasion. Then I heard about Skin Two and went to a few of their early parties and couldn't believe how great the atmosphere was, no one was being pretentious and everyone looked amazing, but I soon grew to feel that there was something missing. So that's why the Torture Garden came about. I'm really into body art and piercing and a lot of former Goths are

now discovering these things, as well as fetish clothing and a new interest in exploring their sexuality.

Louiza, Alan regularly wears rubber and has many friends on the Scene. How about you?

HOUSK

I love seeing people wear rubber but, personally, I'd rather wear something ripped and rotten than sleek and shiny.

LOUIZA

ALAN   It depends on my mood. I go through periods of wanting to look really smart, then I'll drag myself around looking corpse-like and grey and sometimes I just want to be pretty. When I wear rubber it doesn't turn me on, it's just the way I feel like looking at the time — I get a real buzz from people staring at me when I'm wearing something bizarre.

LOUIZA   I prefer leather, especially the smell.

ALAN   I guess if any material could turn me on it would be leather.

HOUSK   You have a whip prominently displayed here on the wall. Do you use it?

ALAN   Hardly ever. It's more for the imagery . . . I like the harder look it gives me when I go out. I've actually only worn it twice. I used to party a lot, I guess I was a tart — promiscuous — but since meeting Louiza I've calmed down — I've even started reading books again.

SEX AND POWER

Nineteen seventy-seven, London. Two female punks stand outside Safeway's on King's Road. Both have short, jet black, spiky hair with blackened eye sockets and lips. One wears an old school blazer festooned with safety pins; the other, a battered biker's jacket. Both wear tiny leather mini-skirts over ripped fishnet tights and stilettos. One girl has a studded dog collar round her neck – the lead attached to this is held nonchalantly by the other girl. The whole thing is meant to shock. And it does.

It is shocking not only to the blue-rinsed little old ladies going into Safeway's but also to the group of hippies who loiter outside the Chelsea Drug Store pub. For here is a new generation determined to kick over everything the hippies represent. Instead of cuddly sheepskins, studded black leather. Instead of love and peace and the Age of Aquarius, anarchy, no future and aggressive posturing. Sexual attitudes, too, have been transformed: where the hippies advocated free love, the punks proclaim, 'We are all prostitutes.' And where the hippies had sought a sexuality of equals – one in which no one dominates and no one submits – the punks, with their dog collars and leads, blatantly celebrate sexual *in*equality.

The hippies' egalitarian ideology may have been well intended but wasn't it also naïve and unrealistic? Isn't someone always on top? Isn't sexual excitement inevitably born within the dynamics of control and the loss of control? And aren't these dynamics themselves contingent upon an inequality of power? Just as electricity cannot exist without both a positive and a negative charge, neither can sexuality. It not only takes two to tango, but one must lead and the other follow. The hippy model of 'love' couldn't handle these facts of life and the resulting soft-edged hypocrisy was a particular source of irritation to the punks.

But while the punks' model of sexuality broke with that of the hippies by acknowledging the power-game component of sex, it also broke with the pre-hippy assumption that such power inevitably resides with the male of the species. The punks' message to the hippies was 'You're kidding yourself if you think that no one is on top,' but by the same token their message to the likes of Hugh Hefner and his fellow playboys was 'You're kidding yourself if you think that thing you've got dangling between your legs automatically means that you're the one who's going to be in charge.'

This was radical stuff but just as the extremist aesthetics of punk eventually diffused into mainstream fashion, so too, I think, did such ideas about sexuality eventually come to influence mainstream thinking on this subject. (Were this not the case it's hard to see how the fetish fashion discussed in the previous chapter could have reached the level of mainstream acceptability, which it clearly has.)

Be this as it may, there can be no argument about the debt that the Scene owes to the punks' sexual ideology. This can be seen both in the decoupling of gender from power which Scene sex takes as axiomatic and also in the extent to which the asymmetrics of power are emphasized symbolically in attire, discussed as a first order of business and equated with personal identity. Indeed, while the labels the Fetish Scene or the S/M Scene are more generally used, it is the slightly more clumsy Sub/Dom Scene that might be said to reflect most accurately the bottom line of Scene sex.

This is evident not only in the number of dog collars and leads found in a typical club but also in the sense in which sexual inequality constitutes a necessary precondition of most Scene sex activities. Obviously S/M is predicated upon a Sub/Dom (or, as the gay and lesbian terminology has it, Bottom/Top) dichotomy and the same can be said of bondage, role-playing, etc. And while fetishism's most obvious objectives might be exhibitionist and sensual, its vocabulary is that of control, power, dominance, submission, restraint and inequality.

Most importantly, while 'lingering' might in theory be a product of simple self-control, its more likely mechanism is the restraining brake of the dominant's power. In all these ways the Sub/Dom dichotomy facilitates the Scene's particular approach to sexuality: take away the premiss of inequality and you are left with the equivalent of a car without a motor. Or, to use the delightful phrase of radical lesbians like Pat Califia or Susie Bright, take away the premiss of inequality and you are left with 'vanilla sex'.

Which is not to say that everyone in the Scene falls easily or per-manently into a submissive or a dominant classification. Certainly there are those whose identity is fully linked with either the Master/Mistress or Slave prefix but there are also those who happily switch from Top to Bottom and back again, depending upon mood or situation. What seems to be universal, however, is a sensitivity to Sub/Dom inclinations (however transient) and an assumption that it is this plus and minus of erotic electricity that powers desire and which makes sexual experimentation possible. What the hippies denied and the punks employed as a shocking symbol has become within the Scene a complex philosophy of 'Topness' and 'Bottomness' which is at once the basis of an erotic language, a brake on instant gratification, an etiquette governing relationships and a core component of personal identity.

If we see Sub/Dom simply as inequality within sexual relations then obviously it is as old as humanity. But this would be an inappropriate definition.

Sub/Dom is a deliberately imposed system of exaggerated, sharply defined, blatantly expressed, in-your-face inequality focused upon, and originating within, the sexual sphere. It is not, in other words, simply the actual inequalities of real life (be they within the workplace or marriage) extended into the sexual field. Neither is it just a bossy, assertive, domineering or, alternatively, a docile, meek, resigned approach to sex.

Sub/Dom is probably best understood as a sort of game – an enclosed microcosm with its own rules and territory – and as such (like the shop floor beating the management at a company football game) it is autonomous from real-life inequalities. (Indeed, perhaps the most typically recognized Sub/Dom situation, the successful businessman paying a professional *maîtresse* to treat him like a slave, precisely inverts the power realities of the real world.) Occasionally the Sub/Dom game is extended into real life with its dichotomies colouring (and thereby eroticizing) the humdrum banalities of making a living or cleaning the house. But even here it is important to note that the sexual sphere's game has been extended into real life rather than the other way around.

It is also important to note that Sub/Dom is a game in which both/all parties are willing participants. This is not the realm of the Marquis de Sade, where victims have no choice in what is imposed upon them and derive no apparent satisfaction from it. The Sub/Dom game is more modern than de Sade's pre-psychological, Machiavellian preoccupations (perhaps slavery and servitude had to become less real before they had appeal as a game?) and its literary exploration had to await Leopold von Sacher-Masoch's *Venus In Furs* in 1870.

Although the title *Venus In Furs* points to this book's fetishistic concerns and although the author's name has become for ever linked with S/M, the most fundamental theme of Sacher-Masoch's famous book is submission and domi-nance. Its central character, Séverin, and a woman called Wanda begin a 'normal' relationship, but Sévérin's belief that there is no equality in love brings an insistence that their relationship develop accordingly with Wanda as the all-powerful Mistress, Sévérin her humbled Slave. Initially Wanda accepts her dominating role only with reluctance but in time she revels in it – to the point of transforming Sévérin into her servant Gregor and requiring him even to wait upon her gentlemen suitors.

Central to all this is a contract that Sévérin and Wanda both sign and which, according to Chris Kraus and Sylvère Lotringer's introduction to the 1989 edition of *Venus In Furs*, is a precise transcription of a pact between Sacher-Masoch and one Fanny Pistor (alias Baroness Bogdanoff):

> She has drawn up a contract according to which I give my word of honour and agree under oath to be her slave, as long as she wishes.
>
> With her arm around my neck she reads this unprecedented, incredible document to me. The end of each sentence she punctuates with a kiss.
>
> 'But all the obligations in the contract are on my side,' I said, teasing her.
>
> 'Of course,' she replied with great seriousness. 'You cease to be my lover, and consequently I am released from all duties and obligations towards you. You will have to look upon my favours as pure benevolence. You no longer have any rights and no longer can lay claim to any. There can be no limit to my power over you. Remember that you won't be much better than a dog or some inanimate object. You will be mine, my plaything, which I can break to pieces whenever I want an hour's amusement. You are nothing, I am everything. Do you understand?' She laughed and kissed me again, and yet a sort of cold shiver ran through me.[1]

Thus does Sévérin become Gregor and thus begins a journey which, while peppered with the occasional whipping, is more an exploration of submission than of masochism. *Venus In Furs* is a timidly convoluted book which provides its author with all sorts of means of obscuring his inclinations behind a smokescreen of historical antecedents and philosophical discourse, but it is nevertheless the first sketch of how a Sub/Dom game might be played. Although its author and the Marquis de Sade have had their names for ever linked by history, it is not a book which I suspect the latter would have understood, let alone approved of, for Séverin both determinedly brings about his own 'misfortunes' and then contrives to derive a bittersweet pleasure from them. (Even if de Sade's Justine might be said to devise her own misfortunes by clinging to virtue, her motive is moral rather than erotic and, furthermore, de Sade's point is that she is a fool for doing so.)

The other great literary exploration of the Sub/Dom game is Pauline Reage's *The Story of O* (1954). While switching the gender of the submissive character, like *Venus In Furs*, *O* also explores the theme of the victim's complicity; it offers two distinct reasons for this complicity. The first is love: O's infatuation for René obliges her to submit to abuse in the château at Roissy where she is used, humiliated, exposed and objectified. She puts up with all this because of her feelings for René and if *The Story of O* ended at this point it would be much less significant. But when René hands over control of O to his friend Sir Stephen (and O agrees to this arrangement) things enter a different domain – for, from this point on, O's reward for her submission is submission itself.

This might appear to be a raw deal, but in O's eyes these rewards are substantial and sublime. We will return to this subject in a moment but for now let us simply note that *The Story of O* defines – more adroitly than any work of literature before or since – the rules and objectives of the Sub/Dom game: the explicit complicity of both parties, the domination and control of one person by another for purely erotic reasons, the wilful abdication of will in an exorcism of self which (nevertheless) initiates a journey of self-discovery.

MASTER KEITH

Keith, you're considered one of the top S/M Masters. How and when did   HOUSK
you start?
I was sixteen and my wife was sixteen as well and, being so young, I   **KEITH**
didn't have a lot of sexual knowledge . . . I could never get her to come.
At the time I didn't even really know what that meant for a woman but I

knew she should have some sort of peak of pleasure and we weren't achieving it. Then one day I tied her to the bed, I was just experimenting, and when we made love she came, so I made the connection: if I tie her up it's better for her.

I made the connection: if I tie her up it's better for her

That's when I first realized there was more to sex than just bonking, there's also mind games . . . mental foreplay. So, now, instead of trying to excite her by just playing with her nipples and fingering her, I began to play with her mind so she could set up fantasies that would help her to orgasm. Now, the lads I was going around with at the time were just interested in whamming it in and shooting their load, carving another notch on the headboard. I'd hear them bragging about this bird or that they'd shagged and how they'd done it in the back of a car in double-time, yet when I was having sex I'd be there all afternoon or most of the evening. We'd be playing and mentally finding out an awful lot about each other, so the word got around and I became quite sought after because I was good at pleasing women.

My wife knew I was going out with other girls but she decided she'd rather be with me than not and so let me get on with it – she knew I would always come back to her. I found out she was deep into this idea of the 'Black Knight' . . . First time I ever heard about that.

Most women settle down with a safe guy, but it's the Black Knight they really want

Most women settle down with a safe guy, but it's the Black Knight they really want, so I portrayed myself as this character and I was also a caring and honest guy. I've never lied to women; they always know right away what I'm about. My girlfriends started bragging to each other about what they'd allowed me to do to

them and I'd hear it from other girls I was just starting to see, too.

Down at the pub there'd be the kind of guy who drinks to boost his courage before he approaches a girl; by the time he tried, he'd be too pissed to do anything. I'd have maybe two drinks all night and a girl on each arm. Eventually I found I needed to chat up dozens of girls to meet one with a high enough level of sexual intelligence and sophistication

who wanted to play the game and I've gone on to know some of them all my life.

HOUSK   Could you explain about being a Master?

The only type of relationship I have is Master and Slave – Sub/Dom. My slave is also my lover, I don't force anyone. Women come to me, ring me up . . . ask if they can come over, I seem to draw them. They'll hear about me from a friend and often write to tell me their fantasy.

Now, if I just played that out they'd be controlling me . . . they don't want that, the type of fantasies they have need me to be in control. Foreplay to me isn't just before sex, it could be a week or a month before. Say a girl rings up and we make a date for a month later, I start right from the phone call. I might post her some ankle cuffs and include instructions for her to wear them in bed, so before she even meets me she's in mental bondage to me. See, at the end of her normal boring day it's me she's thinking of when she plays with herself, because it's new, it's my game . . . and hers. I've planted the seed but she's making it grow, her anticipation gets stronger and stronger.

Since I'm the Black Knight I can move the goal-posts if I want, change the rules, introduce an element of fear, but at the same time she knows I'm safe, not a nutter.

A lot of people think S/M is about hurting people but it's not, it's about pushing certain buttons for long-term foreplay. It's got a frightening veneer but bottom line it's damsel-in-distress versus the Black Knight — who often actually loves his victim.

So a woman needs to feel that, if she's not careful or if she goes too far, I'll hurt her which, of course, isn't true or she wouldn't come to me in the first place, but it's down to me to make it real and stimulating. If I was a sadist I'd enjoy inflicting real pain on my slaves, get aroused by hurting them, but I'm not. I enjoy the knowledge that I'm turning them on like no one else can. They all know if they say the code words 'Mercy, Master,' I'll stop.

I enjoy the knowledge that I'm turning them on like no one else can

I make them vulnerable, tie them in exposed positions and for women who like this — it's not everyone's cup of tea — it gets them really buzzing. Basically my job is to get them to their maximum orgasm and this makes me feel like more of a man. I like to come myself but I'd rather stay mentally sharp and on the edge so I can keep a scenario going successfully.

HOUSK   Are your slaves allowed to leave of their own free will?

KEITH   I've never forced anyone to stay, the door's there. Girls have got annoyed, picked up their bags and walked out, then started crying and stopped at the front door . . . they don't want to leave. I like a happy, relaxed environment so I'll bring them back, find out what was bothering them and iron it out. This is a pleasurable fiction, a mental orgasm not real cruelty.

'Give a thought to your circumstances, think what you are, what we are, and may these reflections cause you to quake – you are beyond the borders of France in the depths of an uninhabitable forest, high amongst naked mountains; the paths that brought you here were destroyed behind you as you advanced along them. You are enclosed in an impregnable citadel; no one on earth knows you are here, you are beyond the reach of your friends, of your kin: insofar as the world is concerned, you are already dead, and if yet you breathe, 'tis by our pleasure, and for it only.'[2]

This is no game. But while queasiness may overcome us as we read the Marquis de Sade's *The 120 Days of Sodom* its logic leaves us untroubled: brute force and coercion explain the victims' presence in de Sade's château. An understanding of their captors' behaviour requires only an acceptance of human nature's dark depths.

It is the inhabitants of another château – that at Roissy in *The Story of O* – who stretch our imagination. Yes, we appreciate that it is O's love of René that initially anaesthetizes her into submission to Roissy's regime. And, yes, we appreciate that Roissy's female inhabitants are frequently bound and chained. But why is there no attempt at escape? Why, when released back into the real world, don't O and her compatriots run straight to the police to tell of their maltreatment? And why when O no longer has the excuse of love does she so look forward to her return to Roissy?

The Sub/Dom game hinges on the complicity of the submissive and yet it is precisely this that seems to fly in the face of logic. Stop people on the street, ask them, 'Given the choice, would you prefer to have power or to be powerless?' and we know what the answer would be. An absurd question. Yet in sexual matters the evidence suggests a very different state of affairs: amongst gay, lesbian and straight Sub/Dom enthusiasts it is invariably the Tops that are in short supply. Fee-charging professionals step in to rectify this imbalance: 'Strict Disciplinarian Accepts Suitable Pupils', 'Toy Loving Bitch Requires Human Toys For Her Games Room', 'Madam Torso The Superior Is Waiting For Contact From All Those Submissive Slaves Out There', 'Bad Habits Corrected Through Convent Education', etc. If the château at Roissy really existed, and if it charged its residents for the privilege of their servitude (particularly if males as well as females were catered for), surely it would be the most over-booked hotel in the world.

What, then, is in it for the submissive? This isn't an easy question and it has no single universal answer. From the perspective of the professional dominatrix – visited night and day by a seemingly endless stream of well-to-do men who pay amazing sums of money to be treated as slaves – the obvious answer is that the experience constitutes a sort of holiday from life's responsibilities. And one doesn't have to be a captain of industry, a judge or a politician to appreciate the logic of this. At any level, making decisions and taking responsibility for them is a burden. In the act of taking charge the dominant provides a release from this burden.

Nor should such responsibilities be seen as purely work-oriented. We live today under enormous pressure to make the earth move whenever we have sex. The submissive, however, happily avoids such pressure. It is the dominant who must propose the route to be taken, and if the journey goes nowhere, it is the dominant who is to blame. If our society is organized so that, typically, it is men rather than women who carry the bulk of decision-making and responsibility, both in the workplace and in the bedroom, then it should come as no surprise that submissive men inevitably seem to outnumber by far submissive women. (And would it not be nice to put this theory to the test by eliminating both of these inequalities?)

Two other theories are often put forward to explain the submissive's motivation. The first is very simple: the submissive craves attention – something which any Bottom can readily acquire in abundance (especially if he or she has sought out a Top with a sense of the theatrical). At a club or at a private party it is common to find slaves displayed and 'presented' – often wearing minimal attire or positioned provocatively – so that all eyes are upon them. The dominant, by comparison, is rarely the centre of attention. The second popular theory suggests that the submissive's motivation derives from a need to expunge some deep-rooted guilt or self-loathing. Generally it is a craving for masochistic physical abuse which seems most obviously aligned to such problems (a subject examined in more detail in the next chapter), but humiliations of a more psychological nature might, arguably, answer the same need. There is an obvious logic to the idea that a desire to lick a dominant's boots or to be urinated upon stems from a sense of guilt or self-loathing. (By the way, some evidence suggests that Sacher-Masoch's delight in humiliation and pain resulted from a guilt born of witnessing his police chief father's violent suppression of a rebellion in Prague.)

There are submissives in the Scene who, one suspects, fit this pattern, but I would not support the view that to be submissive is to be disturbed (nor would I presume that the extent or nature of submissive behaviour necessarily provides an easy guide to whether the motives for such behaviour are pathological). The submissive who seeks a 'holiday' from responsibility or performance pressure seems to me to be acting upon a kind of logic which needn't be defined as mental imbalance (even if the form this holiday might take – being dressed in baby clothes, for example – seems peculiar to most of us).

And neither can O be nonchalantly dismissed as a disturbed personality. We may not wish to follow in her footsteps but it is hard to question her self-esteem or her sanity. There is no hint of any unhappy childhood, no self-loathing and no festering anger or vengeful compulsion. She is attractive and successful in her job. If she has a problem it is simply that throughout her life she has rarely found sex to be as earth-shaking as she would have hoped. (And if this were grounds for bringing in the men in white coats, how many of us would be left at large?) Of course, O is just a fictional character, but I think there are insights to be gained from an investigation of her motives nevertheless.

Essentially what O seeks is the sublime – to be catapulted on to some higher, purer plane of existence. To be sure, this is a sexual/erotic plane (one offering precisely the sort of earth-shaking pleasure that the 'vanilla sex' of her pre-Roissy days never achieved) but ultimately O's quest is extra-sexual, her objectives philosophical, even spiritual. Her thesis is that by submitting to humiliating indignity she will discover in herself a 'sublime dignity' and that by the loss of control over her own actions ('the will that wills self-abandon') she will discover a greater self-hood. ('Was there not a sweetness in acquiring a value through her very humiliation?')

Who can say whether O's rocky road is likely to lead to the sublime end that she proposes (it seems to me that, as in Buddhism, O is seeking some existential place, some point at which the self is defined and energized by its own negation), but what is beyond doubt is that her quest is predicated upon a carefully constructed philosophy and – however bizarre and extreme her submissive activities – it is this which makes it hard for us to dismiss her simply as 'sick'.

Indeed, whatever O's motives, it is hard to dismiss them simply, full stop. O is a complicated character and such complexity seems to be a common submissive trait: the dominant's desire to be dominant not only seems more logical, it is inevitably more straightforward and above board. It is the submissive who is disingenuous – submitting to anything but easy analysis; playing complex games where nothing is ever quite what it seems.

Is it possible that the submissive's true motive is *power*? It is, of course, a truism that the Bottom is always, ultimately, calling the shots: the Top, even if subconsciously, is inevitably shaping her or his game-plan to a knowledge of the submissive's limits, inclinations and demands. In that case how perilously thin and gossamer is the dominant's façade!

And there are other, more profound, forces at work.

Consider the Bottom's unresponsive, unmovable demeanour – calmly complying with whatever the Top may demand but steadfastly refusing to react visibly to, or be fazed by, those demands. In the end, such passivity and unlimited compliance mocks, rather than celebrates, authority, for it denies it its *raison d'être*. In the face of such Nietzschian will, the dominant, all strategies exhausted, is impotent. For, like that famous political submissive Gandhi, the erotic submissive possesses the power to define power as an absurdity.

FRANKO B./PHILIP

HOUSK   What role does S/M play in your lives?

FRANKO B.   At the moment only a small part. We play lots of domination games,

                though. It's difficult to say, really . . . maybe you as an outsider would find

                we do have an S/M relationship.

PHILIP   It colours our daily lives. It goes on all the time as a mental attitude.

We tease each other all the time. Sometimes he goes over the mark and **FRANKO B.**
I'll get annoyed and get him on his knees, slap him, but this isn't during
sex. I'll do this at least once a day if he's naughty, but there's a limit to
how much I can hurt him. Last night when I hit him too hard he got angry
and threw something at me.

A couple of onions. **PHILIP**

As soon as I realized I'd really hurt him — I hadn't meant to, he just **FRANKO B.**
wouldn't obey me — I was sorry. During the day maybe I'll get him on his
knees to suck me but I won't come, we'll just carry on doing what we
were doing before. It's teasing and a kind of reassurance that your
partner still loves you.

So would you consider yourself the dominant one, Franko? HOUSK

Although I think Philip is stronger than me mentally, I rely on my physical **FRANKO B.**
strength, so yes, if I hit him he'll sometimes refuse to make the proper
response and then I'll have to give him an extra one because it wasn't
done properly. This happens maybe twice a day.

More than that. **PHILIP**

Philip, is there an agreement between you to play this kind of game? HOUSK

Well, it just happened. **PHILIP**

You mean you just kind of fell into it? HOUSK

Yeah, I think so. **PHILIP**

He's made me realize I wasn't very good at dominating anyone. **FRANKO B.**

I told him he wasn't firm enough. My punishments and the reasons for **PHILIP**
them weren't definite enough.

See, maybe he'll accumulate eight smacks in one day, but if I do **FRANKO B.**
something bad I'll take twenty out, or, if he's got fifty coming I'll give him
twenty now. That's because he can't take fifty at once.

HOUSK	Are you talking about slaps?
FRANKO B.	Slaps . . . and sticks. A walking stick across the bum. Today was bad because I hit him lower down on his legs, and it really hurt. I guess it was sort of below the belt.
PHILIP	I don't mind getting my punishment if I deserve it but if I feel it isn't fair I get angry.
HOUSK	What does this system do for you?

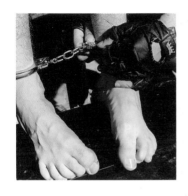

I feel like I'm a slave or servant to a strong uncle or teacher. I like this idea, being very servile and used. **PHILIP**

He gets surprised when he sees I really care for him. **FRANKO B.**

Philip, does Sub/Dom need to be in the context of a relationship for it to work for you? HOUSK

Not necessarily. It does need to be done with a certain amount of affection, though; it makes it better. **PHILIP**

Franko, do you feel like an authority figure, keeping a young boy in line? HOUSK

It's not that he's younger at all, it's the innocence that gets me. At first it was S/M but that's changed. You see, although I'm the dominant one, Philip has more power because he's the one who allows me to do things to him and if he doesn't want to do something he's stronger than me . . . mentally. I mean, I wouldn't push it physically either, really. That might mean the end of our relationship. It's about respect. I'm allowed to exercise power over Philip because he lets me. **FRANKO B.**

Although I'm the dominant one, Philip has more power

Is that the main buzz? The having and giving up of control? HOUSK

Yes. **FRANKO B.**

Yeah, basically. I like to be coaxed, like a dog, sort of, and only punished if I really deserve it. **PHILIP**

Do you like being punished? HOUSK

Oh yes. **PHILIP**

He does! **FRANKO B.**

PHILIP   It's very comforting being told what to do, it's very lovely.

FRANKO B.   We don't plan everything, we just do what feels right at the time. When

you took the photographs you caught us at the beginning of our

relationship, when the excitement was high, but it's not so structured

now.

PHILIP   Our S/M relationship keeps changing. Next week it might be different

again.

If Philip wants me to get down on the floor I will and if he wants to drag me around I'll let him.	**FRANKO B.**
You mean you can exchange roles?	HOUSK
Yeah.	**FRANKO B.**
I'd do it more often but he's stronger than me.	**PHILIP**
I kind of resist sometimes, it depends on how much I want to get him. If I think he's being too cheeky I'll tell him, 'No, I'm doing this to *you* — *you* get on your fucking knees!'	**FRANKO B.**
It's quite nice. I enjoy trying to dominate him but it's even better when he gets his own back.	**PHILIP**
Sometimes he'll try to put a dog collar on me or try to strangle me with the chain so I'll do something I know he doesn't like such as pinch the head of his cock; he really hates it . . . I wind him up.	**FRANKO B.**
Is this fun?	HOUSK
Oh, yes. We're testing each other always, he's almost the brother I never had.	**FRANKO B.**
I feel the same too.	**PHILIP**
I guess we do have an S/M relationship but domination has become more important. The more we get to know each other the further we can push our trust . . . in sex and everything else. Remember, this isn't about hurting someone for the hell of it. There's a code of practice, proper rules to be observed . . . ritual, and the submissive is in control.	**FRANKO B.**
Mmm.	**PHILIP**

How the Sub/Dom game is played – its strategies, techniques, devices, even its technology – is a subject of mind-boggling complexity. This wasn't always the case. In *Venus In Furs* Sévérin's submission is accomplished by the simple device of his becoming a servant, all the trappings and symbolism being borrowed from the already existing institution of domestic help.

In this regard *The Story of O* marks a significant advance. At the château at Roissy there are dozens of female submissives and a hierarchy of valets and masters all engaged in a complex erotic power game. Every intricate detail of this scenario exists to underline and realize the dynamics of sexual inequality. Presuming that *The Story of O* isn't based upon some secret real-life experience, these details must have sprung from Pauline Reage's imagination and one can only be amazed at such inventiveness. Whatever their origins, O's rituals, stratagems and devices have gone on to become a core component of the Sub/Dom vocabulary. There are the identical uniforms worn by the submissives – 'mechanisms for display', which can be hitched up at the front and the back. The carefully crafted leather collars, wrist and ankle restraints with their strategically placed steel rings. The sumptuous, comfortable décor of the master's rooms contrasted with the spartan simplicity of the slave's quarters. The leopard-print hassocks over which the slaves are bent and displayed. The Turkish-style toilets that afford no privacy. The rouge applied to nipples and sexual parts. The ebonite rods in the shape of an erect male member, held in place with chains front and back. The velvet blindfolds. The distinctive whalebone corsets. The master's thin leather gloves. The rules that govern the slaves' behaviour (they may not touch themselves, cross their legs, look directly into a master's face, etc.). The iron and gold rings worn by Roissy's alumni in the outside world to mark their *rite de passage*. The genital piercing and the disc inscribed with Sir Stephen's initials which O wears chained to it. The owl mask which both emphasizes O's nakedness and proclaims her symbolic dehumanization.

These and more are the means by which O's submission is realized. One might have thought that they add up to a definitive, exhaustive catalogue, but a more recent book, *The Story of Gerda* by Jim E. Dickson, demonstrates how Reage's inventions were only a starting point. Gerda's abode is a huge complex of buildings located on an isolated island off the coast of Italy where a veritable army of female slaves ('Servers') are trained in the art of submission. Published in 1982, *Gerda* (no literary masterpiece, unfortunately) is really just a technological update of *O*. Nevertheless, its three hundred tightly packed pages of multi-layered latex garments, bizarre masks, hospital-style décor, futuristic bondage equipment and pleasure-inducing machinery is breathtaking in its exhaustive complexity.

This is Sub/Dom erotic fiction at its most fanciful. Or is it? Practically everything described in *The Story of O* and *The Story of Gerda* can now be purchased by a real life Sub/Dom enthusiast. For example, *The Centurion's Whole Catalogue of the Exotic and Bizarre*, which is readily available in the USA, offers some twenty pages of bondage restraints, twenty pages of state-of-the-art chastity belts (many complete with O's famous 'rods') and an extensive selection of blindfolds, gags, masks, maids' uniforms, battery-operated dildo pants, 'Big Baby' clothes and 'much, much more'.

At the same time, erotic piercing has become commonplace, with skilled practitioners of this body art and a wide range of suitable jewellery readily available. While it is true that most of those who go in for this form of adornment may do so for aesthetic reasons, those who wish to use it for such Sub/Dom purposes are today in a position to convert fantasy into reality. Finally, the strategies and etiquette of Sub/Dom relations have been spelled out in great detail in such books as Terence Sellers' *The Correct Sadist* and Pat Califia's *Macho Sluts*.

Evolving through both fact and fiction, the Sub/Dom game has reached such a point of complexity that one could compile a directory of its many strategies, techniques, devices and technologies; but the following general guidelines should be noted:

(1) The Top and Bottom are differentiated verbally.
('He will at all times address the Superior as "Mistress" or "Master". You may require him to use a variation on this title such as "Divine Queen Goddess", "Father Confessor", "Supreme Being", as you like. He may not use the possessive pronoun, i.e., he may not say "My Mistress" as he is the one owned.' *The Correct Sadist*[3])

(2) Top and Bottom roles are expressed by means of postural differences.
('He may never present himself at full height but remains below the waist or knees of the Superior on his knees or belly. Enjoin him to keep his little paws to himself, at his sides or behind him. No other pose is acceptable.' *The Correct Sadist*[4])

(3) The Bottom is less modestly attired than the Top, or wears restrictive and uncomfortable garments.
('Anne-Marie called to the girls, shouting to them to come down to the garden. All three, like O, were naked. In this house of women, carefully hidden by the high walls of the park and, on the side facing a dirt lane, by shuttered windows, only Anne-Marie and her servants wore clothing.' *The Story of O*[5])

(4)   The Bottom wears a uniform and accessories traditionally associated with servitude.

('Before leaving she takes all my clothes and gives them to the hotel waiters. I am ordered to put on her livery. It is a Cracovian costume in her colours, light blue with red facings, and red quadrangular cap, ornamented with peacock feathers. The costume is rather becoming to me.' *Venus In Furs*[6])

(5)   The Bottom wears the clothes of the opposite sex.

('A pair of ruffled panties does have a universally degrading appeal. As well it saves the Superior from the mild disgust suffered at the sight of the Slave's genitals. For masochistic women a soiled pair of men's jockey shorts serves the same purpose.' *The Correct Sadist*[7])

(6)   The Bottom is put in bondage.

('The brass bed had been stripped of its mattress and bedding and on the frame two bed-length boards had been fixed and covered by a rubber sheet. Released from his waist shackles, the man with the blue eyes placed himself on the covered wide boards, his head on a small pillow and, using more brass chains, I padlocked him to the bed rails, his wrists above the level of his head, his legs spread wide.' Helen Henley, *Enter With Trumpets*[8]) ·

(7)   The Bottom is prohibited from/rendered incapable of speaking, or wears a blindfold or a mask.

('She was dressed in her skin-tight latex suit, booted and gloved, with a steel belt encircling her small waist and a wide steel collar covering the bottom of her latex hood. As usual, she was gagged. She minced across on high stiletto heels, carrying a breakfast tray.' *The Story of Gerda*[9])

(8)   The Bottom is either obliged to experience orgasm or prohibited from doing so.

('There was a soft humming noise, and next instant she felt the vibration of The Machine against her, nosing against the rubber as it sent waves of pure ecstasy through her tortured body. Shame and humiliation and raw desire washed over her, and she tried to cry out to stop this monstrous, subtle addition to her torment.' *The Story of Gerda*[10])

(9)   The Bottom is used as a piece of furniture, or treated as an animal.
('It was truly an extraordinary sight, these tiny carts pulled by pony girls. Shapely legs pumped up and down, faces straining with the effort. We were all shouting encouragement from the terrace . . . The tip was good, after two laps of the garden, number three romped home. She was quickly released from her sulky and hugged her jockey . . .' 'A Day at the Races' by Mike Vickers in *O* magazine[11])

(10)   The Bottom's body is ritually pierced, tattooed or branded to indicate permanent ownership by a master.
('"On the blank side," said Anne-Marie, "your name will be engraved, also your title, Sir Stephen's first and last names, and, beneath that, a device: a crossed whip and riding-crop. Yvonne wears a similar disc on her collar. But you'll wear yours on your belly . . . Show your belly, Yvonne." The red-haired girl rose and lay down on the bed. Anne-Marie opened her thighs and had O notice that one of her labia, midway down and close to its base, had been pierced: a clean hole, such as a ticket-puncher makes.' *The Story of O*[12])

Such a list could never be definitive but it doesn't matter because in a sense all such Sub/Dom devices have now been eclipsed by something new: the Scene nightclub. It is one thing to play out Top/Bottom games in the privacy of your own home (or, indeed, your own château), quite another to do so with hundreds of strangers watching you. Pauline Reage realized this: O's final appearance at the Commander's party is especially erotically charged precisely because her submissive condition is so publicly displayed. Take away all those strangers' eyes and O's long journey is denied its climactic finale.

One wonders if Reage ever imagined that such scenes would become a reality, but this is precisely what the Scene is: a stage where private erotic power-games can be played out in a semi-public context. Because of the turbo-powering effect of such mass voyeurism, even subtle demonstrations of sexual inequality may generate a level of erotic *frisson* which extreme Sub/Dom activities might not achieve in private. Never before have people been able to play out such games so publicly without fear of provoking consternation or even arrest. Today if you live in London, New York, San Francisco, Paris, Amsterdam or Berlin – and many other major cities – you can find a club in which you can exhibit yourself openly as a slave or a mistress/master, something which Sacher-Masoch's or Reage's generations could only fantasize about.

If Sub/Dom were not a game, if it were simply inequality within sexual relationships, such voyeuristic feedback would be irrelevant. But it *is* a game and, as in any spectator sport, its potential for generating excitement is at least as dependent upon the fans as the players – for they too serve who only stand and watch.

Nineteen ninety-four, London. Two women stand by the bar in a club called Submission. One wears a tight corset, a G-string, stilettos, rings in piercings in her nipples and a dog collar. The other wears a sleek, shiny rubber catsuit, stilettos and nonchalantly holds a lead which is clipped to the other woman's collar. A few friends stop by to chat. The woman in the catsuit tells her Slave to fetch everyone drinks. To make things a little more interesting a pair of handcuffs are clicked over the slave's ankles. Everyone in the crowded bar takes note of her tiny, mincing steps as she makes her way back and forth from the bar in her precarious stilettos, her bare bottom and her ringed breasts swaying provocatively throughout the operation. Her task completed, she kneels in front of her mistress; in one hand she holds her mistress's drink, in the other, an ashtray. In this position she hears the conversation going on above her while her eyes come to rest on the leather riding-crop which dangles from her mistress's belt and which provides such an opportune introduction to our next chapter.

VEIN/FRAN

Vein and Fran are both dominant but agreed to try to submit to one another,

with Housk as a witness.

Would you like to talk about what just happened?   HOUSK

I didn't like it when Fran put the handcuffs on me. I'm always dominant,   **VEIN**

FRAN I've never done that before. All I was thinking was how I couldn't wait to be free and putting the handcuffs on Fran. Then I just got flustered again.

FRAN Yes, when it was my turn to be submissive it was OK for a few seconds but I've never had chains on me or a dick in front of my face before. I wasn't happy about it at all.

VEIN I thought chaining Fran up would be a brilliant thing to do, but that she'd never let me. I mean, on her knees with me wearing a strap-on! You surprised me, Fran.

FRAN I wanted to find out what it would be like, and it was good to try it because I know Vein knows what she's doing, but no way would I do this with anyone else.

VEIN This is the first time I've tried to find out what being submissive is like with a woman and I completely panicked.

FRAN Do you remember our first time? I was so drunk, you had me in a club and the next morning I found bruises all over my nipples. I thought, I can't see this mad woman again – she hurt me!

VEIN Fran didn't ring me the next day, she just ran away, and I'd thought she was really hard. When I finally saw her again she just said, 'I'm dominant and so are you, so what's the point?' Well, I secretly think I'd like to be submissive sometimes, in fact it's my big dream. The trouble is I'm such a controller and it's hard to trust someone enough. I let Fran try tying me up one night in my house, just some light S/M, and I blanked out for a bit – broke free and scratched her face and I don't even remember doing it. I came to in another part of the room with Fran holding me saying, 'It's me, Fran, don't worry, it's all right.' It was weird.

'I'm dominant and so are you, so what's the point?'

HOUSK So what role do you think S/M will play in your relationship?

I just don't know. When Vein was using the whip on me it was quite soft **FRAN**

but I know what it means so I kept thinking, no, I should have the whip in

my hands.

Well! **VEIN**

What part did S/M play in your lives before you met each other? HOUSK

A regular part. I'm good at it if I'm not involved with someone. I can be **FRAN**

hard and give pain, and I love to do it.

HOUSK	What's pleasurable about it for you?
FRAN	It's a physical thing, I actually shake inside . . . it's great.
HOUSK	Why is it easier or better for you outside a relationship?
FRAN	I hold back if I care for someone, I can't really hurt the one I love.
VEIN	For me, it's not necessary to have an S/M relationship to fulfil my sexuality, though I've always had a cruel, demanding streak. A long time ago I was sexually submissive so I could learn the techniques and understand what it was about, but I was only submissive in the bedroom and when I learned what I needed to know, I left him. I do know physically and psychologically where I'm taking someone in a scene and that's very important.
HOUSK	Fran mentioned shaking inside, how about you?
VEIN	I don't shake inside but it is very different from conventional sex. It's like orchestrating something. You know where you're taking someone and where they've been, it can be transcendental — very intense, almost destructive, and very creative at the same time. I also think it can be quite addictive, what with the hormones released, the endomorphins. There's also the temptation to push things further and further, to see how far you can go.

It can be transcendental — very intense, almost destructive

HOUSK	Do you believe that it's the submissive who has the power?
FRAN	Yes, absolutely.
VEIN	Also, submissives are usually manipulators and pains in the arse — the dominant ends up with all the responsibility.
FRAN	My ex used to deliberately wind me up so I'd give her rough sex but if you let them get away with it they take the power and you lose control, so I'd get angry but then walk away. They always try to push your buttons.

Submissives work on reaction rather than interaction or even action. I
was beginning to become this very reactive, violent person. When I'd
snap, my previous girlfriend's eyes would light up because she'd
brought me to this point.

It's like, 'Show me how strong you are, prove you're dominant.'

Vein has said she's found she can be violent. How about you, Fran?

Very, when it's necessary.

VEIN

FRAN

HOUSK

FRAN

VEIN   I don't think I'm as violent as Fran, but I've been discovering this side of
              me more lately. The trouble is I snap and blank out and don't consciously
              know what I'm doing and I find that scary.

HOUSK   Are you able to separate that violence from your S/M or does it spill
              over?

VEIN   I think a lot of people would like to say that it's different but how can it
              be? You're the same person and I've yet to meet a passive, easy-going

dominant sadist. I would say I'm more dominant than sadistic because I'm not that violent . . . well, not as violent as Fran or other people I've met.

Does the violence in Fran attract you?   HOUSK

No, that's not what drew me to her, it was her dominant personality. I like **VEIN**
the way Fran can take care of herself.

I'm not violent all the time, either.   **FRAN**

HOUSK	So what attracted you to Vein?
FRAN	She was different. At first it was physical because she doesn't look like the other dykes, and then I realized she wasn't stupid.
VEIN	Thanks!
FRAN	But it's true, and I can say these things to her.
VEIN	When I first saw Fran she had a Mohican, Gothic make-up and heels so she was quite tall and I thought, 'Look at that!' The friend I was with made a beeline for her and stuck her tongue down her neck — typical dyke behaviour, they're all so cruisy. When I saw her again I still thought she was great, but really quite sweet.
FRAN	I am!
VEIN	Then I became really sexually attracted to her. When we actually started talking and having sex I was shocked because she was so in control.
HOUSK	Have either of you ever been in a dangerous situation because of S/M?
FRAN	Just once. I was doing a scene and everything was going great when I suddenly noticed my partner was greeny-white and bleeding and shouting, 'Stop!' because she couldn't breathe. I hadn't been aware of how far I'd gone, I'd sort of tranced out. I called a doctor and had to explain what had happened and luckily she was all right. I discovered it gave me a lot of pleasure to do this so I have to control this tendency. I like to be on top of things always and that's what really scared me . . . I'd actually lost control.
VEIN	Nothing like that has ever happened to me while doing S/M. I once hurt someone a lot, physically, in a fit of anger, but that wasn't a sexual thing.
HOUSK	Do you think S/M is a permanent part of your lives?
VEIN	Definitely, it's part of me.
FRAN	I've been interested since I was seventeen — I don't think it will change.

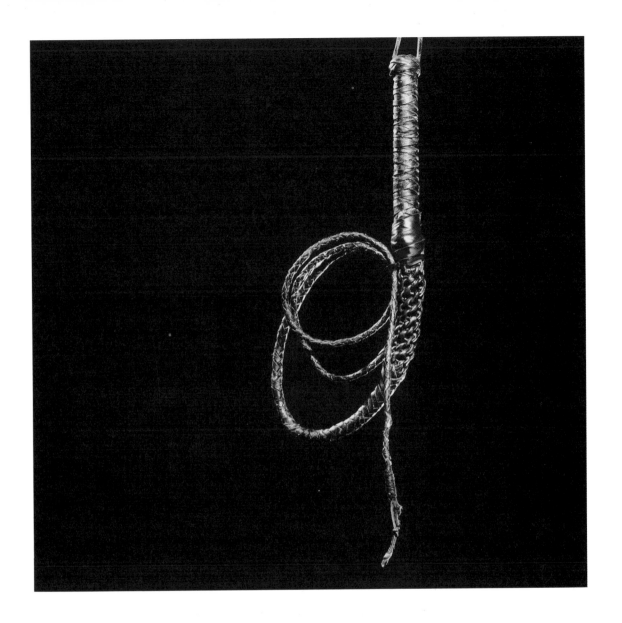

PLEASURE AND PAIN

To most of us pleasure and pain appear to be irreconcilable opposites. Life is full enough of discomfort and torment and we seek to mark off the territory of sexual experience as a pain-free zone. Accordingly, S/M seems an illogical as well as a disturbing proposition.

In particular, it is the masochist – delighting in that which a seemingly sane person would do anything to avoid – who challenges the pleasure principle which has become such a keystone of our modern, secular culture. The Medieval flagellant or the Mexican pilgrim scraping bloodied knees on stone steps *en route* to the Virgin of Guadalupe are not of our world – they inhabit a time and a place in which people willingly sacrificed earthly pleasures for some greater reward. The sexual masochist lacks even such theological justification, and phone-box stickers advertising the services of some whip-wielding Madam violate not only the phone company but also that philosophical foundation of modern life – hedonism.

Although some recent S/M enthusiasts have sought to redefine it as 'sensuality and mutuality', as everyone knows, S/M derives from the juxtaposition of those strange bedfellows, the Marquis de Sade and Leopold von Sacher-Masoch. In fact, neither of these gentlemen precisely fits the modern notion of S/M. De Sade because he wasn't able to distinguish between a consenting masochist and a victim; Sacher-Masoch because (despite what his name has come to signify) his central preoccupations seem to have been Sub/Dom power games and fetishism rather than pain-oriented S/M.

That said (and it is an important distinction), it is undeniable that Sacher-Masoch's submissiveness was tinged with masochistic tendencies. For example, in his correspondence with Emilie Mataja he writes:

You would give me very great pleasure if you'd send me a good photograph of yourself. I would be even more delighted if you allowed me to visit you in Vienna and if you were willing – in furs, of course – to whip me.[1]

While such references to pain are surprisingly rare in Sacher-Masoch's novels one can imagine him fitting into today's S/M Scene (provided, of course, he could find a Wicked Wanda with no qualms about wearing fur!). The same, however, could not be said of de Sade. Never fitting into his own turbulent times, de Sade's brand of sadism would leave him just as estranged in the 1990s, and the reasons for this lie at the heart of what contemporary S/M is and isn't.

The most glaring problem is of course the fact that de Sade's fictional victims are *victims* rather than consenting masochists. But the problem is also more subtle, hinging on the lack of any possible mutuality between those on either end of the whip. De Sade's world is a one-way street – the victim has no voice, no presence, no reality – and such unilateralism would be unacceptable in the S/M world that today bears his name. (True, Justine has a 'voice' of sorts but de Sade's whole point is that she deserves only contempt for her propensity to end up on the cutting end of the whip.)

A useful comparison might be made between de Sade and Pat Califia, a well-known contemporary lesbian writer and Top. Califia leaves neither her readers nor her Bottoms in any doubt about her position:

I am basically a sadist and have no interest in body worship, domination, French maids, or bondage unless these activities can be combined with physical pain.[2]

But unlike de Sade (or at least his characters) Califia's full and proper title should be 'S/M sadist' – that is, one whose actions and desires operate within a continual interface of opposing polarities. As she puts it, 'A good Top has to listen to the voice of the Bottom within',[3] and she asks, 'How can someone who has no idea what it feels like to be physically restrained or hurt know the value of what the Bottom is giving them or calculate how much "punishment" to dole out?'[4]

This is responsible and denotes a level of concern which those outside the Scene might not anticipate, but the difference between Califia's brand of S/M and de Sade's more primitive sadism goes further. The women on the receiving end of Califia's whip are her *partners* – they are both in it together, however transitory their relationship and however different their sexual profiles. Like any self-respecting S/M Top (lesbian, gay or straight), Califia wants the Bottom to have a voice, to be a real and unique person. This is not so much a moral issue (although I'm sure it has such a dimension) as an erotic one – sexual excitement being generated not only by polarity but by the interface between polarities. It is precisely the lack of this which makes de Sade's writings so tedious to read.

This is why SM is more accurately represented like this: S/M, than like this: S&M. The modern S/M Scene isn't just a bunch of sadists dishing it out to a bunch of consenting masochists. The giving and the receiving of pain are seen as two components in a reciprocating, interactive *system* – an erotic Yin/Yang, which if typography permitted would have an 'S'-shaped demarcation indicating a symbiotic interdependency. While not all S/M sadists would agree with Califia's advocacy of 'switching', I expect that all would agree that they and their masochistic partners constitute two inseparable sides of the same coin.

This dynamic reciprocity lies at the heart of S/M and it structures all of its philosophy and actions. First and foremost, such reciprocity couldn't exist without mutual concern and respect. And it is these three fundamental tenets of the S/M Scene – reciprocity, concern and respect – which make the stereotyped public perception of such activities so erroneous. S/M is not about partner-bashing, assault, wanton physical or psychological destructiveness – or, indeed, any of the 'mindless violence' which has unfortunately become such a common component of modern life. While it has been argued that the growing popularity of S/M reflects the growing everyday violence of our lives (and at least as logical a case can be made for S/M as an *antidote* to this violence), it is indisputable that S/M and common-or-garden violence are as different as chalk and cheese.

Most obviously, as Carol Truscott says in her essay 'S/M: Some questions and a few answers', 'Sadomasochism is about *consent*. Violence is about coercion.'[5] This distinction is clear and inviolate throughout the S/M world: consent is the key without which the dungeon door remains firmly bolted. This fact of S/M life, however, brings us back full circle to the question with which we began this chapter: why should anyone consent to pain? And, as with the question of why someone should choose to be submissive, it has no single, definitive answer.

Not all submissives who allow pain to be inflicted upon them are masochists. A submissive may not 'get off' on pain but will accept it (and consent to it) as part of the package deal of being a Bottom. This seems to be the case in *The Story of O* where periodic whippings occur but where such events do not come across as specifically erotic or orgasm-inducing.

As I suspect was the case with Sacher-Masoch, O's real delight is in being controlled by an Other. The specific things that are done to her within this structure aren't really important. What matters and what arouses is her acquiescence. Her pleasure is in serving her respective masters – if they choose to whip her it may be because it excites them to do so, because they view this as an essential part of her training or because they require this as 'proof' of her submission. (For, after all, a Bottom who received only pleasure from a Top would be exhibiting scant evidence of submissiveness.) Accordingly, if there is pleasure in pain in such circumstances, it is what might be termed 'referred pleasure' – its true source flowing from deep in the power plays considered in the previous chapter.

There are also, of course, those who consent to and actually seek out pain for its own sake. It is the motives of these, the true masochists, that seem so profoundly enigmatic to the rest of us. The psychoanalysts from Freud to Reik have their answers to hand: masochism is 'normal' aggression turned in upon the self rather than directed outwards towards some other person. Or, pain is a price to be paid in order to overcome some deep-rooted guilt associated with sexual pleasure. All such theories have in common the presumption that the masochist is a disturbed or 'sick' individual, and doubtless some masochists fit this pattern, but a number of recent authors have put forth 'positive' theories of masochism which seem to me to be intriguing and worthy of consideration.

The most scientifically based of these theories hinges upon recently emerged evidence which suggests that pain can trigger the release of opiate-like chemicals in the brain which have the effect of producing an endorphin high. This has been recognized with regard to individuals who break through a 'pain barrier' after jogging, lifting weights or doing aerobics. Accordingly like many exercise fanatics the masochist can be categorized as an endorphin junkie.

Carol Truscott's 'S/M: Some questions and a few answers' puts forward this theory and it is developed more fully by Geoff Mains in his essay 'The Molecular Anatomy of Leather' ('leather' being a code word for S/M-related activities in the gay world). After guiding the reader through the jargonistic jungle of brain chemistry, Mains' conclusion is as startling as it is concise: 'Quite simply, pain is not enjoyable because it is a second-rate substitute [for pleasure], it *is* pleasure.'[6] If this is correct then we are confronted by a fascinating irony – the masochist as hedonist.

A slightly different but, I think, related point has been made to me in conversation with masochistically inclined acquaintances and friends. Pain activates, revs up and kick-starts the nervous system and this has the effect of supercharging any subsequent pleasurable sensations. Whether as a warm-up routine to heighten sexual pleasure or as pleasure itself (as in the Truscott/Mains theory), such masochism seems slightly undeserving of its name.

A second 'positive' theory focuses on S/M's apparent capacity to induce trance-like states within which the participant is catapulted on to a higher level of consciousness – a condition which in a religious/spiritual context is traditionally labelled 'ecstasy'. Here one discerns a parallel not only with the Medieval flagellant or the bloodied Mexican pilgrim, but also with those native American Indians who participated in the O-kee-Pa ceremony or Hindus who take part in the Kavandi ritual, both of which involve the piercing and suspension of the body.

Such historic and cross-cultural evidence of an inherent link between pain and spiritual awareness gives credence to the view that at least some S/M masochists are in it for cosmic rather than hedonistic reasons. If this juxtaposition of the erotic and the transcendent seems strange to us it is only because our Judeo-Christian heritage (at least in modern times) disallows such a possibility. For centuries the eastern Tantric cults demonstrated the viability of the opposite view.

S/M's capacity to open such doors of perception might derive from the simple operation of the opiate-like brain chemicals which we have already considered. However, both my reading of S/M literature and my background as an anthropologist point me towards the view that at least as important a part could be played by the ritualistic structuring of S/M experience. The power of ritual has been largely forgotten in our modern world and we have been rendered spiritually impoverished by this neglect. Ritual structures action, focuses attention upon meaningful symbols, slows down time and sets an event apart from the everyday. Most of all, those who participate in a ritual event become more than the sum of their parts – a community – and this together with ritual's other qualities means that extraordinary things can occur within its domain.

By modern standards, S/M is exceptionally ritualistic. Almost as inviolate as the rule of consent is the requirement that nothing should be done casually. Everything must be done *right*, according to the rules, in good time, within the correct atmosphere, with due respect for ceremony. That magical forces might be unleashed in such circumstances should come as no surprise. It doesn't matter if a ritual's immediate purpose is rain-making or orgasm-making; for reasons no one fully understands, whatever is approached ritualistically can become magical.

Practically all the contributors to Mark Thompson's valuable book *Leatherfolk* testify to the magical, transcendent power of S/M ritual. The essay I like best is Tina Portillo's 'I Get Real: Celebrating My Sadomasochistic Soul', which concludes:

> The very shape of my consciousness changes, and all negative thoughts are driven away. Afterwards, I always feel awesomely peaceful and relaxed, loved and lovable. No other high can match or surpass it. It makes me feel so totally alive, and *all there* – as opposed to *numb*.[7]

CLARE/BRIAN

HOUSK   Brian, what do you do for a living?

BRIAN   I spent many years in the dental industry and then, later in life, my daughter and I started a venue-finding service for big conferences.

HOUSK   When did you discover your interest in corporal punishment?

BRIAN   Very early on. My earliest masturbation fantasies were of dominant women.

HOUSK   At what point did you become involved in the Scene?

BRIAN   I wanted to pursue my fantasies as soon as possible and hired a professional lady when I was seventeen in 1948. She lived in Mayfair

I hired a professional lady when I was seventeen in 1948

and had a marvellously equipped dungeon. The first time I went she sent me upstairs to wait and the minute she walked in the room I had an orgasm. The session was almost over before it began but then she said, 'I'm now going to beat you for having an orgasm before I've allowed it,' which was excellent.

HOUSK   Can you describe what you get from being beaten?

BRIAN   It's changed over the years. When I was younger and more virile I'd have an orgasm while being beaten. I can no longer do that, I'm in my sixties, but I still enjoy being beaten and now I try to increase my threshold of pain. If I take a good beating I'll try to take more the next time.

HOUSK   What if you want to stop?

BRIAN   Madam and I have a let-out word, which you'll find most couples on this Scene do for safety reasons, mine's in Dutch, so if I say 'No, no, no . . . I can't take any more!' Madam won't take a blind bit of notice, but if I was

to say our special word I trust her to know I mean it. I haven't said it yet
and I don't plan to. Sometimes I've gone too far because I know if I say it
the first time the second will be that much easier and I've got a huge
sense of pride, as Madam can tell you!

Does having a solid relationship enhance the S/M for you? HOUSK

Personally, I don't think it makes any difference, but the beauty of it is BRIAN

that I have met the right lady who is not only very good at what she does

for me but is completely trustworthy. You see my lady could hurt me at any time just by jabbing a knife between my ribs but that's not what S/M is about. Because of the amount of punishment I can take I wear a kidney belt. You have to be sensible and protect those parts of the body liable to permanent damage. Madam doesn't want to cause me permanent damage any more than I want to receive it.

HOUSK   Have you always been careful or have there been any mistakes?

A mistake has been made, yes. I've had one serious bit of damage. A lady who thought she knew what she was doing tied me up against a wall and then kneed me in the groin. I had to go to hospital and eventually one of my testicles was removed because of the damage she'd done. That sort of pain is not what S/M **BRIAN**

is about.

What part does corporal punishment and S/M play in your life? HOUSK

A major part. Aside from my work, which I enjoy very much, C/P and S/M **BRIAN** occupy my free time. If Madam is out I'll use a magazine or video and go into my fantasies. Although I love the lady I'm with I still need my fantasies to achieve orgasm.

Do you have other types of sex? HOUSK

Yes, we practise penetrative sex as well as S/M. In fact, we've been **BRIAN** together so long we tend to have S/M sex only at parties, not when we're on our own.

Is there anything else you'd like to say? HOUSK

Yes, I love long whips on my back. They're delicious. When I feel the **BRIAN** skin on my back tightening as a result of a good beating I feel a contentment. The next day is just gorgeous – a great inner contentment.

Now, Clare, when did you discover your abilities to dominate? HOUSK

Well, it started in a funny way. In 1967 I met a man in a coffee bar in **CLARE** London who started seeing me. He eventually confessed he wore stockings and suspenders under his clothes, which I found extremely amusing. He took me to a barbecue held by the Mackintosh Society.

He eventually confessed he wore stockings and suspenders under his clothes

Everyone was standing about dressed in rubber and I thought it was smashing. There were two photographers and they got me to put on a rubber mac, open face hood and gas mask. They took lots of photos and when they sent them to me I was very amused.

Next I got a letter from a man who had started a break-away club from the Mackintosh Society, because he found them too tame and when my friend from the coffee bar wanted to take me I got him to buy me a rubber dress . . . my first rubber dress! Then in 1978 I went to the first Rubber Ball in Hammersmith Town Hall with a well-known actor I was seeing who was mad about rubber and I couldn't believe it, all these kinky people! I was in my element. I met this marvellous couple and we all went back to my actor friend's Mayfair apartment and had a rubber orgy, it was fantastic! We put the man, a bank manager, in the bath in a rubber suit and gave him water sports, he was beside himself in sheer ecstasy. Anyway, his lady inherited a black book and started doing professional domination and that's how I got started. We first did double domination sessions; I was broke and it was good money. I remember a week-long party in Yorkshire where I ended up being the special treat. I was fitted with a nice butt plug and rubber knickers. Suffocation techniques were tried on me and then I was told to cane another girl. I hadn't done this before so I was hesitant but after being told she had a *TV Times* down her knickers I tentatively began. Well, I really got into it and discovered for the first time how much I enjoyed doing it. It gave me a great buzz and I was good at it and I still am ten years later. As far as Brian and I are concerned, we've got a slight problem – his bottom is ruined. His right cheek bursts open if I

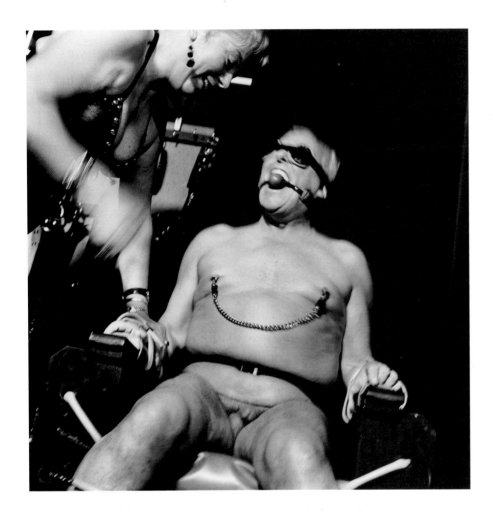

bend him over and start whacking him and there's blood everywhere. So
we have to leave his bottom alone these days.

What does caning give you?   HOUSK

Power! It's also good for releasing aggression from the system. It would   **CLARE**

do the average person a world of good to try it occasionally. It's like

cushion-beating.

Do you find it better in the context of a relationship?   HOUSK

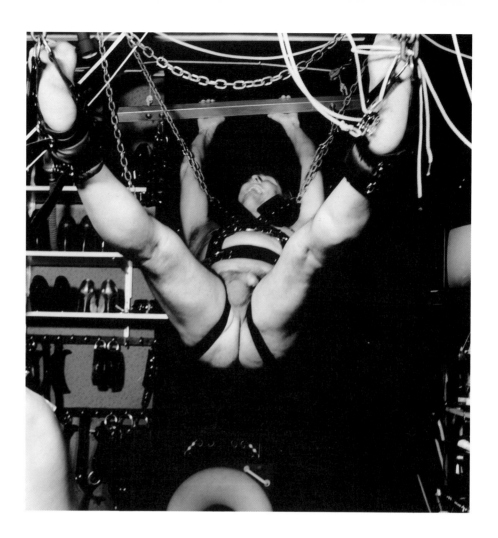

CLARE No, it doesn't matter. A bottom's a bottom, a cane's a cane and the bigger the bottom the more fun.

HOUSK Do you enjoy sex without S/M?

CLARE I enjoy sex with the partner of my choice, oh yes. S/M and sex do and do not mix. There's an element of sexiness in it but, as you get deeper into S/M, straight sex isn't so exciting, something's missing. Also since I'm dominant I feel the male should be doing all the pleasing: I demand, I get — in theory.

Would you say S/M is a major part of your life? HOUSK

Absolutely. It's taken over. In my late teens when I got married I was just **CLARE** a little girl from the North who was brought up the usual way. If I angered my northern husband he'd verbally chastise me, whereas if I'd been who I am now, I'd have swiped him off the face of the earth. I've definitely become more aggressive with age, especially towards common men, they're so stupid.

Have you always felt this way? HOUSK

It's become more obvious with age. I've always felt men's brains were **CLARE** between their legs.

Is there anything else you'd like to say? HOUSK

Yes. A lot of men come to me with their fantasies and if I really fulfilled **CLARE** them they'd be horrified, it's all in the mind. So . . . it's better to travel in hope than arrive in despair.

In 1987 four home-made videos were seized by the police in Bolton, Lancashire. These videos had been made by a group of homosexual S/M enthusiasts for their own use (they were never sold or distributed). These videos were reported to contain scenes of an extreme nature:

Penises are carefully nailed to boards. One is repeatedly lacerated by a scalpel until it disappears in a wash of blood. Map-pins are pushed with surgical precision through a scrotum; match-heads are attached to one man's nipples and then lit; a sharpened nail is pushed into the head of a penis and then extracted as blood spurts from the wound. A young man's initials are branded on to his lower stomach with a piece of wire heated in a blow-lamp.[8]

The tapes were passed on to the Obscene Publications Squad which launched a massive investigation under the code name Operation Spanner.

Subsequently, over the course of two years, 'about 100 people – all homosexual – were interviewed, 42 were arrested, and 16 eventually committed for trial at Lambeth Magistrates Court'.[9] When the charge of conspiracy to corrupt public morals was added to that of assault, the case was switched to the Old Bailey (although this additional charge was dropped almost immediately after the trial began).

The men who had participated in the S/M scenes recorded in the Spanner videos never considered that they were breaking the law. The 1967 Sexual Offences Act states that homosexual acts in private between consenting adults are within the law. All the men were adults and all were fully consenting.

At the Old Bailey, however, Judge James Rant ruled that such consent didn't matter because 'the courts must draw a line between what is acceptable in a civilized society and what is not'.

Accordingly, '11 men received sentences of up to four and a half years for assault; 26 others were cautioned for the offence, thought to be unique, of aiding and abetting assaults on themselves'.[10] The tabloid press loved it – 'Jail For Beasts in Vile Gay Sex Orgies'.

In February 1992 the case went before the Court of Appeal. While the sentences were reduced (for example three years to six months, four and a half years to two years) the convictions were upheld. In ruling Lord Lane commented, 'The satisfying of the sado-masochistic libido does not come within the category of good reason'.

The initial verdict coupled with this appeal verdict would appear to have set a legal precedent with significant and wide-ranging implications. As Jon Savage argued in an insightful article in the *Observer*:

> This ruling has effectively tightened legal control over the body: SM sex which involves the breaking of the skin is now effectively illegal, as is body piercing where sexual pleasure and intent is involved. An ultimate application of the judgment would make other sexual activities like spanking and even the giving of love bites illegal, although a prosecution on this basis is highly unlikely.[11]

The outcome of the Spanner case causes concern in a host of different ways.

First, there is the damage that this trial and its attendant, often hysterical, publicity has done to the perception of S/M in particular and alternative sexuality in general. There has long been a tendency to use S/M as the generic label for all forms of kinkiness. This isn't in fact very accurate (the majority of those attending a fetish club may have little or no interest in S/M in the strict sense of the term). Such labelling is also unfortunate because it means that the 'perversity' most likely to cause the maximum disquiet is given the highest profile. Throughout the Spanner case and its appeals, even quality newspapers such as the *Guardian* and respectable TV programmes such as *Newsnight* interspersed material about men mutilating each others' genitals with material about, for example, Skin Two's Rubber Ball fashion event. It seems inevitable that such coverage promotes the impression that everyone who is into the Scene is *ipso facto* into S/M.

Further, within the sub-section of the Scene that does practise S/M the percentage who are likely to participate in such extreme activities as those reportedly practised by the Spanner defendants must be very small – perhaps infinitesimal. S/M's magical efficacy lies in its use of ritual structure and symbolic nuance, with the result that a little bit of actual pain can trigger significant erotic effect.

The S/M enthusiast who finds it necessary to participate in what most people would consider extreme acts, is, in my view, suffering from a lack of imagination. Most S/M enthusiasts are highly imaginative and creative in their approach – emphasizing the mental rather than the physical in their search for erotic and personal fulfilment; getting off on the sublime and finding no need of the ridiculous. Yet in the light of the publicity surrounding the Spanner case I suspect that the public perception must surely be that everyone who wears rubber or leather must be into 'S/M', and everyone into S/M must enjoy having nails driven through their genitals at least once a week.

If a concern with what is essentially an image problem seems trivial, it does have a serious aspect. With the shadow of AIDS hanging over us our society should be encouraging people to consider non-penetrative, alternative sexual strategies. Sub/Dom game-playing, fetishistic sensuality and S/M (*sans* blood-letting) are essentially 'Safe Sex' activities. Spanner – by further encouraging the idea that S/M is a generic label for all forms of kinkiness, by emphasizing the most extreme forms of S/M, and by apparently criminalizing S/M – has impeded that expansion of sexual possibility which constitutes one of our most effective counters to casual, virally risky sex.

Just as worrying are the legal issues which Spanner raises. Within the legal profession there is concern at the way an obscure case from the 1930s (in which a man was found guilty of assault for caning a woman for purposes of 'sexual gratification') was used to establish a precedent in such a contentious and far-reaching issue. As Mrs Clare Brakspear, JP, has commented: '. . . that such behaviour should come within the ambit of criminal law without reference to Parliament is cause for alarm to this law-abiding citizen'.[12]

More broadly, Spanner's legal precedent raises serious questions about our dominion over our own bodies. It is this point that has been focused on by many of those involved with Countdown On Spanner, an organization which seeks to bring the implications of this case to public attention. For example, the writer Adam Mars-Jones has commented:

> 'The rulings set a precedent whereby we don't own our own bodies. They make us children. Our bodies have been confiscated – to be leased back to us on certain conditions.'[13]

And as S/M activist Kellan Farshea asks:

> 'If we control nothing else in this society, surely we control our own bodies?'[14]

This issue was even more directly challenged in the separate but related trial of Alan Oversby who in his professional guise as 'Mr Sebastian' is one of

Britain's most respected practitioners of the art of body piercing. Although not personally involved in the incidents that first triggered Operation Spanner, Mr Sebastian's name was apparently linked to some of the defendants and it was decided to prosecute him for his body-piercing activities. (This, despite the fact that all of his clients were obviously consenting and despite the fact that none complained about his services.)

Because of my background as an anthropologist specializing in the subject of body decoration I was asked by Mr Sebastian's solicitors to write a report outlining the history of body piercing throughout the world. In it, I emphasized the antiquity of this form of adornment, its wide-spread cross-cultural occurrence, the importance of facial piercings to various traditional ethnic cultures within Britain and the essential part which all forms of body decoration play in personal and social expression. It was and is inconceivable to me that a modern state's legal system could even be contemplating restricting an individual's right to transform the appearance of his or her own body. Such 'customizing' of the body is something which human beings have been doing for as long as there have been human beings and one could even argue that it is this that most clearly differentiates us from all other living organisms.

At the conclusion of the Mr Sebastian trial, the judge's ruling established a distinction between body piercing for aesthetic and decorative reasons on the one hand and piercing for sexual or sadomasochistic reasons on the other hand. Mr Sebastian pleaded guilty to falling into the latter category in one instance and was given a fifteen-month suspended sentence.

Facial and body piercing is arguably the most rapidly growing form of adornment in Britain today. Most of those who acquire such decorations say that they do so for aesthetic reasons. It is generally recognized, however, that many piercings (such as those on the genitals or the nipples) can have the effect of enhancing sexual sensations. Does the Mr Sebastian ruling imply that the many thousands of people who today possess such piercings are breaking the law? Or, if someone has an ear piercing and they acknowledge that toying with it can be a turn-on, does this qualify as a criminal act?

All societies seek to control the appearance and the sexuality of their members. This is especially true of tribal and peasant societies where thousands of years of tradition are brought to bear on individual freedom. Modern society, however, has long sought to protect the rights of the individual. As Mars-Jones, Farshea and other Countdown On Spanner members have suggested, one would have thought that an individual's own body and his or her consensual, private sexual behaviour should reside deep within the domain of personal rather than state control. Both the Mr Sebastian and the Spanner trials suggest otherwise.

I personally find distasteful the extreme S/M activities which the Spanner defendants apparently indulged in. I wouldn't want to see friends of mine doing this sort of thing to themselves. Furthermore, there are some hypothetical questions in my mind regarding the possible validity of 'consent' where the person giving that consent might, for example, be mentally retarded or seriously disturbed. (But surely this is a matter for the medical profession rather than the law courts? As I understand it, Britain already has legal provision for bringing people into care if they are thought to be a danger to themselves.) Finally, it does seem to me that (especially in the light of AIDS and hepatitis) a good argument can be made for a law requiring body piercers and tattooists to be licensed and subject to public health checks. But such concerns pale into insignificance when put up against the legal and personal implications of the Spanner/Mr Sebastian trials.

Immediately, there is the problem of enforcement. Are we to have police officers and/or video cameras positioned in every bedroom in the land to ensure that love bites and playful bottom spankings don't get out of hand? Presumably not, but the alternative is also disturbing: enormous discretion on the part of the police in selecting who to target in the application of such a wide-ranging and ill-defined legal precedent.

Which brings me to a final but crucial point: while tribal and peasant societies rely on the informal judgement of elders to keep individual inclinations in check, modern societies rely on written laws and these require in turn a great sensitivity to linguistic meaning. Good laws use words that have precise and agreed meanings. Bad laws use words that defy definition. In my view the judge's rulings in both the Mr Sebastian and Spanner trials fall into the latter category.

If the difference between legal and illegal body piercing hinges on a distinction between 'aesthetic' and 'sexual' motivations, how are these words to be defined? My *Concise Oxford Dictionary* defines 'sexual' as 'of or relating to sex'. The pertinent definition under 'sex' also gets us nowhere: 'sexual instincts, desires, etc., or their manifestation'. I began the text of this book with the question 'What is sex?' and, as the whole of the first chapter demonstrates, it has no easy answer.

When Lord Lane upheld the guilty verdict of the original Spanner trial in the Court of Appeal he ruled that 'The satisfying of the sadomasochistic libido does not come within the category of good reason'. What is and what isn't 'sadomasochistic libido'? The *Concise Oxford* defines 'sadism' as 'a form of sexual perversion characterized by the enjoyment of inflicting pain or suffering on others' and it defines 'masochism' as 'a form of (esp. sexual) perversion characterized by gratification derived from one's own pain or humiliation'. What, then, is 'pain'?

Typically we assume that this neat little word must have a straightforward, objective meaning. We assume that our bodies are dotted with tiny receptors marked PAIN and, alternatively, PLEASURE but this is not the case. It's all in the mix, in the mind: personal, culturally conditioned and impossible to quantify or measure objectively. Furthermore, and immediately relevant to any attempt to legally demarcate the 'sadomasochist libido', pain and pleasure seem to be mutually reciprocating sensations.

Even in the most 'vanilla-ish' of sex the boundaries between 'pleasure' and 'pain' are hard if not impossible to identify. Indeed, all forms of pleasure seem to require some level of tension or what in isolation might well be categorized as unpleasantness. To put this in non-sexual terms: those strident violins in Beethoven string quartets or the discord of a Coltrane sax solo cut us to the quick. Yet without such 'unpleasantness' would the eventual resolve which Beethoven or Coltrane offer be so satisfying? Isn't such 'pain' the key difference between great music and the saccharin sounds pumped into elevators?

Or, to use another metaphor, how much pleasure would there be in eating if we eliminated all that is bitter, sharp and bordering on the unpleasant? Chillies, pepper, endive, saffron, lemons and – dare I say it – unsweetened vanilla are all the sort of 'acquired tastes' that defy easy classification within the boundaries of the 'pleasantly pleasurable'. And what about hot curry? Isn't curry a culinary delight which ventures into a realm that might be termed gastronomic S/M? Perhaps some sort of benchmark could be established to define just how hot a curry could be before it became an instrument of assault. Perhaps the police could be issued with little machines with which suspect curries could be objectively scrutinized.

The luxury of such objective demarcation isn't, however, feasible in the case of sexual S/M. How exactly is that law enforcement officer positioned in our bedrooms going to know the point at which the pleasure/pain divide has been breached? By listening to seemingly agonized moans? By observing contorted facial expressions? The mix of pleasurable pain and painful pleasure which lies at the heart of sexual experience will always defy the phenomenological precision which the law now apparently requires.

If it were in my power I would give to the Spanner defendants the gift of imagination that they might in future obtain profound delights from less drastic torments; to Judge Rank and Lord Lane a vanilla pod, that they might suck it and see pleasure's perverse possibilities – and that they might recognize that the civilization which they seek to protect could not exist with only the bland leading the bland.

Kevin, when did you discover you liked S/M?   HOUSK

I came across it through a friend in 1975, in cartoon books. A few years   **KEVIN**

later I started going to some of the early fetish clubs, and then, as a

parting gift, the foreman of a building site I was working on gave me a

copy of *120 Days of Sodom* by the Marquis de Sade. Finally, about a

year ago, I started to go to fetish clubs again with Fizz and that's when I first actually did it and I haven't stopped since. I'd always been into it, though; when I used to make love I always held down and gripped the arms of my partners.

FIZZY   When I was fifteen I used to love the romantic adventure novels in which women were forever being captured, tied up and sold to harems, but the first time I ever saw it was in Kevin's cartoon magazines, which he kept

in his flat. Then one night Kevin and I went out with some friends to a
nightclub. In walked a man and woman, she had no knickers on, and he
was leading her on a dog collar and chain. When they reached the bar
she knelt on the floor at his feet, they were right next to us, and I said,
'Kevin, look at that — we could do that!' It was amazing.

So now that you do S/M what do you find appealing about it?

Well, I get orgasms and I never used to have them.

HOUSK

FIZZY

HOUSK	Is that because of the physical reality or the mental stimulation?
FIZZY	Both. It's not often that the physical reality doesn't match up to my expectations.
KEVIN	I don't get very much from it emotionally because I'm not a very emotional person, but I find it fascinating.
FIZZY	So what does keep you involved, then?
KEVIN	I suppose I get off on the domination. It used to be kidnapping teenage girls when I was a teenager.
FIZZY	What! In fantasy or reality?
KEVIN	Well . . .
HOUSK	So at the moment do you have definite Sub/Dom roles?
FIZZY	We did but we breached that border the other night actually.
HOUSK	So you're becoming flexible?
FIZZY	Definitely, he encourages me. I was frightened I'd lose sight of the dominant side of him but I haven't.
HOUSK	What particular element is most important to you?
FIZZY	Dressing up. If I don't feel my appearance is right I don't get off, but if it is, then I can just forget about it and enjoy myself.
HOUSK	Is that because you're allowing a different side of yourself to appear and be expressed?
FIZZY	Yes, absolutely.
KEVIN	I like it all — though I think I get more out of the feedback from Fizzy than anything I generate myself.
FIZZY	We had three days in Bristol recently where I was tied up all the time and it was fantastic but by the end we'd wrung it out, so to speak, and it was time to move on to something different.
KEVIN	We don't have definite scenarios that need to be acted out.

If we're not having S/M sex then we do tend to use one of two scenarios. Either he seduces me and spends a long time stroking and exciting me or he just goes for it and I let him — the two extremes.

FIZZY

GENDER PLAY

Sex is a comparatively recent invention. For most of the history of life on our planet reproduction was asexual, and evolution – dependent upon the mathematically unlikely event of useful genetic mutations – proceeded slowly, imperceptibly. Sexual reproduction had the advantage of reversing the odds, making it almost impossible that an offspring would precisely resemble either of its parents. Such variety is the stuff evolution is made of.

The logic of gender is less straightforward. To produce the kind of variety which evolution requires, it is necessary only that two separate individuals mix and match their chromosomes. Why then divide a species into two distinct genders? The development of 'lock and key' genital apparatus at first glance seems to suggest an answer but not all sexually reproductive and gendered organisms possess such equipment. Also, why not simply equip *all* individuals with both a 'lock' *and* a 'key'?

Such a solution, however, would require not only the duplication of genital equipment but also the duplication of every organ involved in the reproductive process – so we can see the advantage of gender as a reproductive 'cost cutting' exercise.

In addition, by dividing a species into separate genders the business of mating can be ritualized into an orderly routine whereby the male/female does such and such to kick things off and the female/male responds accordingly. Without such a system of gender-defined roles mating would be hopelessly confusing, time-wasting and stressful.

In all species except our own, gender roles in mating rituals are programmed instinctively (and for this reason are identical throughout a species). *Homo sapiens*, uniquely, define gender roles and structure mating rituals within a given culture with the result that these differ from society to society or (in the West where change has been more rapid) from one era to the next. We *learn* what it means to be a male and what it means to be a female and mating rituals are part and parcel of this learning experience. The only thing that is universal in all human experience is the existence of gender itself – there is no such thing as a 'unisex' society.

Whether our own society will succeed in creating an exception to this rule is debatable but it is certainly true that within only a few decades we have participated in a remarkable and unprecedented experiment. Even back in the early sixties when I was entering adolescence, the gender-specific rules of mating were remarkably well defined and inviolate by today's standards. Males invited females on a date, paid for everything, provided transportation and at appropriate moments made their moves (arm around the shoulders, hand on the knee, 'French kissing', attempted bra removal, etc.). Females also made moves but these were of a different kind, involving the non-verbal medium of gesture, posture and dress. It was a complicated business but one had only to learn the rules to know how to play the game.

The 'Unisex Revolution' of the sixties sought to sweep all this aside. In mating, as in disco dancing, you would henceforth 'do your own thing', regardless of gender. The proposition had much to commend it: the roles of men and women in the workplace and in the home were in transition and it was logical that these changes should be extended to the mating game as well. Also, the changes proposed by the Unisex Revolution offered women a degree of sexual activeness which had previously been denied them.

And while women would benefit from an opportunity to step outside the passive 'sex object' status to which they had traditionally been confined, the inverse would do men a world of good. As we have seen, since the time of the Industrial Revolution men in Western society had been perversely denied a delight in 'dressing up' and flaunting themselves as objects of desire and (while less often commented upon) this too was an unhealthy state of affairs. In short, the Unisex Revolution raised the possibility that both men and women might be more fulfilled and complete in themselves.

Nevertheless, it must also be said that it was a remarkably naïve project. If human beings throughout history have used male/female roles to structure the mating game there are sound reasons for this. Namely, that such sign-posting of appropriate behaviours minimizes confusion, saves time and reduces the stress involved in what is inherently a taxing experience. The Unisex Revolution dismissed existing gender-based roles but it offered little to put in their place. You can 'do your own thing' on your own, in private, but for two people to do their own thing *together* requires some sort of co-ordination.

It is possible that such problems could have been largely overcome if communication skills regarding sexual interest and intent had grown more sophisticated, or at least more honest and direct. Certainly, back in the late sixties and early seventies, the wearing of T-shirts and badges with sexually suggestive messages ('Make Love Not War') constituted a crude attempt at communicating a pro-sex stance but typically such signals were too generalized to be effective – broadcasting to all and sundry rather than narrowcasting to certain types of people.

Nevertheless, if the problem had only been one of communication perhaps solutions would have been forthcoming, but history threw a much more intractable spanner into the works. The Unisex Revolution only *half* happened and this has left our culture in a state of almost total confusion as regards sexual relations between men and women.

We live in a world where some people continue to subscribe to the view that there is no useful distinction to be made between the sexes; some people completely dismiss this as absurd nonsense, and the majority seem to be positioned somewhere between the two. In such a situation no one – male or female – knows how they should proceed in sexual matters. No one knows what roles they should play or what rules apply and it is hard to imagine a situation with a greater propensity for generating indecision and stress. Certainly no animal species could reproduce successfully if faced with such confusion in sexual signalling.

Our failure as a culture to resolve the unisex proposition one way or another has precipitated a gender crisis which permeates all aspects of our lives. To give one simple example: should men open doors for women? I know women who expect and enjoy such courtesies but I also know women who define such behaviour as chauvinistic. The result is that something which should be straight-forward has become problematic for all concerned. And if today men and women experience confusion over such simple matters is it any wonder that sex – a stressful business at the best of times – has become a minefield?

We have become the strangest of creatures. Like other animals we possess the physiological markings of gender but for us such signals no longer convey any clear meaning. Using sexually provocative styles of dress and body decoration, we often amplify these signals (as if simply pumping up the volume would get the message across) but while, for example, a bright pink posterior on a female gorilla means 'I am on heat/I'm sexually available/Go for it', today's provocatively displayed (female or male) posterior offers no such behavioural directions. As Philip Norman put it in an article entitled 'Sexual Signals':

> Most creatures on earth express sexual intent by a signal or message which, however bizarre, is instantly recognizable and unequivocal to others of the same species. And for many centuries human beings followed this sensible principle. . . .
>
> In Britain in the nineties, those signals have become confused and contradictory beyond any logical interpretation. So uncertain are we about the messages being given to us and our own proper response, so greedy and yet fearful, so satiated and yet starved, that it's a wonder the whole business of procreation does not grind to a full stop. Turning to us from the sane sexual order of wolves or stick insects, David Attenborough himself could do no more than throw up his hands in bafflement.[1]

And so we stand around on the dance floor of desire unsure not only who is to lead and who is to follow but even if we should tango, foxtrot, disco on our own or retire to the bar for a drink.

While heterosexuals today have physiological markers of gender but few clues as to their meaning, gays and lesbians possess no gender differences with which to structure their mating rituals and relationships. This is obvious but it does nevertheless serve to make an interesting point: in functional terms, a sexual/gender signal which has no shared meaning might as well not even exist and accordingly 'straight' people today must increasingly operate sexually within a situation that is not unlike that encountered by gays and lesbians.

Faced with the problem 'Who does what?' gays and lesbians have tended to use explicit visual codes of dress and adornment which are designed to define roles and to signal sexual interests. For example, many gay men place a handkerchief in either their left or right back pocket to indicate whether they are 'active' or 'passive'. Placement on the right = passive while placement on the left = active; the colour of the handkerchief can also indicate a predisposition for certain sexual practices. (Traditionally, lesbians have used 'Butch' and 'Femme' style differences to define their respective roles and inclinations but this appropriation of heterosexual gender differences has increasingly been questioned and it is Top/Bottom style signals which are in the ascendant.)

Such distinctions are discussed in 'Sex and Power', and it is interesting to note how heterosexual participants within the Scene seem to have looked to the gays and lesbians for inspiration. The reasons for this are obvious: first, the Top-Active/Bottom-Passive distinction offers a signalling system which, unlike 'I am a male'/'I am a female', actually *means* something in the sense that it indicates sexual orientation and provides clues for an appropriate behavioural response. Second, Top-Active/Bottom-Passive signals and roles offer the possibility of structuring sexual relations in ways which respect feminist values – implying, 'Yes, I recognize that sex is a power game, but, no, I do not recognize any intrinsic relationship between male-ness and power.'

This is a very neat and useful solution to a seemingly intractable problem and it suggests an obvious answer to the question 'Why is the heterosexual "Scene" becoming ever more popular?' But more than this, it indicates the extent to which the Scene constitutes a valuable research facility for mainstream society.

When Philip Norman suggests that 'it's a wonder the whole business of procreation does not grind to a full stop' he is not guilty of exaggeration. But while he simply goes on to outline the extent of the problem, the Scene proposes a solution: we need roles to structure sexual behaviour but let us decouple those roles from gender. This has implications both for initial, across-a-crowded-room signalling and also for the structuring of sexual roles within established, stable relationships – providing a language which partners can use to talk about those things that might otherwise be unsayable.

While outside the Scene the 'gender crisis' continues to sink heterosexual men and women into a mire of mutual fear and suspicion, inside the Scene there is both clarity of intent and the possibility of avoiding altogether the issues of genital determination which even 'New Men' and 'New Women' seem unable to resolve.

As the broader heterosexual community comes to consider the viability of Top/Bottom roles, as I'm sure it will, the objection will doubtless be raised that such a distinction is too clear-cut, too clinical, too reductive of affection and desire to the status of a power trip. And, yes, it would be tragedy if love should come to be seen *only* as a question of 'Who's on top?' But neither is there virtue in a blinkered, naïve and romanticized belief that power has no part to play in sexual desire and loving relationships.

Sexual roles and mating rituals must by their very nature entail at least temporary inequalities of power. What has become problematic in our age (and, to my mind, rightly so) is the assumption that biological gender defines sexual politics. Our society has long since passed the point where the question 'Who's on top?' can be answered according to who's got what particular genital apparatus. We must de-gender sexual power or accept that the battle of the sexes is a war without end.

BJ/HAZEL

HOUSK	BJ, when you do your nautical number, what role are you playing?
BJ	A male sailor, a pansy one – a sailor boy, really.
HOUSK	Hazel, would you like to talk about the sexual excitement you get from being photographed?
HAZEL	I feel more free shagging BJ over a table with a camera present,

because how we look becomes more important than what we're feeling.
We've done this once before on video. We made our own porno film
from a scene in *Querelle* where a sailor gets fucked by this big black guy
over a table. BJ got fucked by me up the arse and my girlfriend filmed it. I
got so excited that I came in the first twenty seconds! My girlfriend
couldn't stop it, I came too fast. She was meant to do the next fucking
scene but she was up the stairs and out of the house as fast as she could

run and we're going 'Oh, oh – we went too far!' See, as long as we were just going through the motions it was OK, but the minute we extracted any real pleasure it was no go.

HOUSK   Are sailors your only turn-on or are there others?

BJ   My recent one is the Mitchell Brothers from *EastEnders* – I've got a car mechanic's outfit, a cowboy one . . .

HAZEL   All your imagery is taken from the realm of gay men.

BJ   I suppose, to a certain extent. I guess if I was to emulate a straight man I'd be the worst one you could meet, a real selfish bastard sexually.

HAZEL   The kind that comes all over you then wipes his dick on you.

HOUSK   What do you get from having that attitude as a man?

BJ   It's hard to describe because when I start behaving like that it takes over really quickly.

HAZEL   Maybe it's because you know from the other side how good that feels. To be used is such a beautiful feeling, it's right next to being needed. There's a complete freedom from responsibility. So once you're aware of that you can use it without guilt to turn on someone else . . . Of course I mean this in the context of consent and choice, not dragging someone you don't know up an alleyway. That would be rape. I think there should be a different word to describe rape or abuse in a consensual sexual context. If someone *agrees* to let you show up at any time, break in, hold a gun to their head and fuck 'em, it isn't actually rape any more. You see, people who don't understand S/M and heavy role-playing view it from a wrong perspective. We're actually taking charge of and responsibility for our sexuality and maybe if more people had a legitimate outlet for working their needs and aggressions out, less real crap would occur.

What part does S/M play in your lives?   HOUSK

I would say it's in every part of our lives, right down to washing dishes in   **HAZEL**

black rubber gloves.

You see I work with it and so does she . . . it's everything.   **BJ**

Having said that, my favourite sex is vanilla sex when I'm in love.   **HAZEL**

So do you prefer your sex with love?   HOUSK

Well, we differ on this. I just have the best orgasms when I'm in love.   **HAZEL**

BJ   I don't think I could ever be in love, I think trust is more important. I can do anything with someone I trust. When someone says 'I love you' it freaks me out because that's fine, and all, but do they fucking trust me or is their head in the clouds? I won't just drop my drawers, I need trust.

HOUSK   Could trust be your term for what others call love?

BJ   Exactly, that's what it is, I like the term better. Love gets so twisted and can mean so many things whereas trust is trust, end of story.

I'd like to clarify something: I don't consider myself an S/M dyke, I'd call myself a sexual pirate because I do what I like. Following through on sexual adventures is what I'm about. **HAZEL**

If I had to be categorized I'd say I'm a dyke but if I'm being turned on it doesn't matter, it could be a man or anything, I'll go for it. **BJ**

What about dildos, what does the penis mean for you? HOUSK

I'd love one – to experience really going into someone – but I'll be content with the fantasy. **BJ**

When I first slept with women it was done as a total denial of dick, I'd already slept with lots of boys before. Since those early days I've had a change of heart, partly because of the change in the social and political climate, but mainly because I'm more at ease with myself. **HAZEL**

I guess I was lucky. I was raised by my parents and two gay uncles. I knew lesbians from an early age and two men or women kissing was OK, it wasn't an issue. As for S/M, both my parents were into things like that so, again, it wasn't a problem. In fact what society calls normal I find peculiar. **BJ**

M/F   Tick one.

What could be simpler? X/Y chromosomes. Internal/external plumbing. Lock/key. Biologically it all seems so pleasantly straightforward. Tests can be done in the lab. What's the big deal?

But, of course, gender identity *is* a big deal – something beyond chromosomes, plumbing and laboratory testing. Something which mocks our culture's obsession with scientific clarity. Something which challenges us to see ourselves and the world differently.

What is 'masculinity'? What is 'femininity'? Is the New Man simply a figment of the media's imagination? Is Today's Woman really so different from her mother or grandmother? Can a woman run a multi-national corporation or be sexually assertive and still be 'feminine'? You can't open a magazine or newspaper without coming across such questions. Everyone is desperate for some answers, some guidance. And yet we seem to be no closer to understanding gender identity than we were twenty years ago.

It isn't only that our definitions of 'masculinity' and 'femininity' are in flux; more fundamentally, our understanding of gender itself is being transformed. These days it is much more widely accepted that 'masculinity' and 'femininity' are cultural constructs – something that anthropologists and social historians have long appreciated. For in a world where gender is constantly being redefined this conclusion is inescapable.

This is all as it should be but this new understanding of gender also opens the floodgates of possibility. If 'masculinity' and 'femininity' aren't simply an entailment of chromosomes or genital equipment, if they are a cultural construction, then what definition of these terms can we usefully create for ourselves? While such invention is exciting it is also daunting.

As with so many other things, the Scene is a place of great experimentation regarding the problem and the possibilities of gender identity. In a club like the Torture Garden one encounters so many people of indeterminate gender that one can begin to think that gender confusion and possibility are things that are somehow confined to this particular sub-culture.

This is of course not the case. Where the Scene differs from the Real World is simply in its openness – its insistence that things should not be swept under the carpet, its willingness to let people be up-front about their inclinations and confusions. Our whole society is in the grip of a gender crisis and while the Scene's openness and experimental daring may provide us with a valuable background to a discussion of gender identity today, the implications of such a discussion extend far, far beyond the boundaries of this particular laboratory.

In a sense, all experimentation with gender identity both within and beyond the Scene can be broadly categorized as 'gender bending'. However, within this generic glossing there are actually several completely distinct means of coming to terms with gender which need to be identified: there is the transsexual, the transvestite and the angel, and each comes to the 'M/F Tick One' problem from a different perspective and with a different objective in mind.

The transsexual is someone whose core gender identity is at odds with his or her biology. Consider the case of Mahnitta:

> When I was three, I became aware . . . I thought . . . I should have been born a girl. And
> I regularly used to cry myself to sleep because there'd been a terrible mistake. I'd started

cross-dressing by the time I was five – wanting to be feminine and not a little boy. But just because of this bit of flesh between my legs, I had to behave like a man and act a certain way. So for a long time, I felt life was a permanent limitation on my ability to be myself.[2]

Why should such a 'terrible mistake' have occurred? Throughout Europe only a few hundred years ago it was thought that such mistakes were the work of mischievous fairies who amused themselves by stealing the souls of newborn babies and relocating them in other babies' bodies. Today we have science to propose more prosaic explanations. According to one theory, transsexualism:

starts prenatally when sex hormones start to affect the brain. As is known, all embryos, even those with the male XY chromosomes, begin by being female. In the case of boys, the Y chromosome activates the male hormone testosterone to masculinize the foetus. In some cases, however, there hasn't been enough testosterone to masculinize the brain, so that although a physically normal male, the boy may be convinced he is 'really' a girl. With female-to-male transsexuals, the brain, but not the body, has been affected by too much testosterone. According to this theory, not accepted by most geneticists, something has gone wrong with the sexual wiring-up of the brain at a crucial stage of development . . .[3]

To me, such a theory seems too reductive and, in the end, unnecessary. Freud was right about some things: our personalities, our essential selves – our 'souls', if you will – are largely formed at a very early age. Typically one would expect 'This is a boy' or 'This is a girl' to shape infantile experience towards those personality traits which fit comfortably and 'naturally' within the society's definition of the appropriate gender. But other factors may alter early-life experiences so that the essential self develops characteristics (e.g. pronounced passivity or, alternatively, aggressiveness) that are at odds with the current cultural expectations of biological gender.

But whatever the cause – prenatal chemistry, early-life experiences or mischievous fairies – the more pressing problem is how the transsexual should deal with the mismatch of body and spirit which has occurred. In the West, beginning in the 1920s, scientific and surgical advances offered a previously unimaginable solution: alteration of the body to allow it to correspond to the inner self's core gender identity. Inspired by such well-publicized examples as the travel writer Jan Morris and the tennis star Renée Richards, this became the accepted, obvious solution for many thousands of male→female transsexuals; a solution that previous eras would have thought simply beyond belief.

Unfortunately, the parallel option of female→male surgery has not yet achieved the same level of success. Although phalloplasty (the surgical construction of a penis) was attempted as early as 1936, even today the results are generally not considered to be either cosmetically or functionally satisfactory. Often there is abdominal scarring and an inability to urinate, and the surgically created penis may require the insertion of a rod if an erection is to be achieved. Worse still, in some instances penises created by phalloplasty have simply fallen off – resulting, not surprisingly, in 'massive castration anxiety'.

Some have argued that the reason for this lack of success is simply that surgeons are not really applying themselves to the task at hand; perhaps because male surgeons in our 'phallocentric' culture just don't want to contemplate the possibility that man's best friend and most precious possession can be so readily constructed. While this may seem like obsessive paranoia on the part of biological females who want to gatecrash the citadel of manhood, suspicions are raised when considering another dilemma faced by the female→male transsexual: typically they are rejected for surgery because, as Marjorie Garber says in *Vested*

Interests: Cross-Dressing and Cultural Anxiety: 'they often are not considered psychotic enough or distressed enough for treatment, since wishing to be or act like a man is considered 'normal' or 'natural' in this culture'.[4]

But let us imagine a future time when all transsexuals could have and regularly do have their bodies adjusted to comply with their core gender identities. Is there no cause for hesitation about such a prospect?

What worries me about such a scenario is the implicit assumption inherent in any surgical solution that gender and genitals are one and the same thing. Have we not as a culture begun to break through such physiological determinism? Have we not really taken on board the idea that 'masculinity' and 'femininity' are *cultural*, *historical* constructions which can themselves be altered? Can't we at long last allow the possibility that gender identity might float free and independent of genital endowment?

Interestingly, as Garber points out:

After the boom in transsexual surgery in the seventies, there is some evidence that those who once looked towards surgery for the solution to the conundrum of sexual identity are considering other options.[5]

Other options?

MARINA/GILES

Giles, when did you start cross-dressing?

I've been doing it most of my life, since I was four. I don't really know

what I get from it. I'm not trying to be a woman, although I can feel very

feminine. It's not even the thrill of the forbidden because I've always

done it. I feel more powerful in women's clothes. I think I look better in

HOUSK

GILES

them because I have the kind of figure that is complimented by dresses and corsets.

MARINA   The first time I saw Giles like this was after I'd come to his flat the first time – he came out in a corset and stockings! I remember being surprised but thinking this must be a very interesting person; something just clicked. I didn't feel sexual about it, it was more like Giles had something to give me. You know, if you asked me out of the blue what kind of man I like I'd say macho men, powerful men, but I've never actually been out with one.

HOUSK   So maybe that's just a fantasy.

MARINA   I think you're right. All my boyfriends have been very feminine and Giles is the best of all. He hasn't got any hang-ups about wearing women's clothes whereas my other friends who dress like this aren't really comfortable, you can tell they're hung-up about something. Giles is very sensitive and doesn't try to bully me. Whenever I'm upset and I need some feminine understanding, Giles can give it to me. It's like magic.

GILES   I think all men are potentially like me, it's just that society polarizes us. Macho men aren't so strong really, because they've usually denied their emotional, intuitive side, which makes them frauds on some level, incomplete.

MARINA   I come from a traditional Italian home and still I knew my mother was the head of the family even though my father was physically stronger.

GILES   I've always thought women were stronger.

HOUSK   Would you like to talk about bondage?

GILES   I've always been fascinated by enslaving other people. When I was little I used to crawl into the kitchen, get bits of string and tie up the legs of my mother's female friends. My mother never commented, which is quite

strange in itself, but I remember it vividly. I also used to tie myself up in the bedroom after I'd cross-dressed. I was never interested in the usual childish games the other kids would play, I'd stay alone in my room exploring my sexuality — masturbation, anal penetration, cross-dressing — I never felt bad about what I was doing.

Do you consider yourself dominant or submissive?

Dominant, I can't bear to be punished or restrained.

HOUSK
GILES

HOUSK   Marina, when did you discover this side of yourself?

MARINA   When I started going out with Giles. We had normal sex for a few weeks then, one night, he started playing this game with rubber gloves, a whip and handcuffs. I was helpless and he started to insert things into me. I really liked it but I thought it was weird. He spent hours exploring and playing with my body and no one had ever done this before. Do you remember, Giles? It's developed since then and now we don't have conventional sex very often. Sometimes we'll even go weeks without doing anything but then all of a sudden . . . whoosh! We get off on me displaying myself, maybe in a restaurant, and that can be enough to keep us happy for a while. I always project this dominant image and I am, but I

We get off on me displaying myself, maybe in a restaurant

love being tied up and submissive with Giles. I really trust him. I'm not into pain, just bondage, and only by Giles. Having said that, I enjoy whipping people in clubs but as an amusement, not a turn-on. I also like people telling me I'm beautiful and kissing my boots, especially if Giles is watching.

And I can always stop it if I think it's going too far.

So you remain in control?

Yes.

I like that, Giles doesn't even have to say anything, he doesn't even have to be in the room and I know. That's what I mean by being on the same wavelength; I know when he feels I'm going too far.

GILES

HOUSK

GILES

MARINA

The Transvestite is a much misunderstood creature. It is generally assumed that anyone who dons the apparel of the opposite sex must be homosexual and yet transvestites who are heterosexual in orientation are much more common. While the camp, over-the-top drag queen may offer the most striking example of cross-dressing, the more likely case is the 'straight' suburban man who furtively borrows his wife's lipstick and knickers.

Another widely held popular assumption is that the transvestite is transsexual but this too is a fallacy. While the transsexual wants to switch genders (or has actually made this transformation by means of surgery), the TV wants – if only symbolically and transiently – to embrace *both* the masculine and the feminine. This is the 'Phallic Woman' who delights in the surreptitious erection concealed within the folds of supremely feminine attire. Or this is the 'Vaginal Man' who, while getting off on the accoutrements of masculine attire, has no intention of switching genitalia.

The transvestite, in other words, is greedy – wanting both masculinity and femininity, unwilling to choose. In this sense s/he is a hermaphrodite.

In the erotic sci-fi novel *The Change* (by 'Willie') this concept is taken literally by the character Erson who, although eventually transformed into Ursula both in terms of genitalia and appearance, opts to retain her cock, arguing, 'Who said you can't have it all?' and answering herself, 'Hell, I just want everything!'

But while Ursula's 'omni-sexuality' may raise all sorts of fascinating erotic possibilities, it also obscures a proper understanding of transvestism as it is practised in real life. Gender is a culturally constructed universe of meaning and behaviour which is encoded in an aesthetic style. It is this symbolic universe rather than mere genitalia that the transvestite appropriates – a way of being rather than a way of fornicating.

Why should someone wish to do such a thing? Perhaps a more reasonable question is 'Why should someone *not* want to do such a thing?' For like Mount Everest, the opposite gender is 'there', beckoning to us, inviting us to wonder why a vast territory of experience and meaning should be off limits to us. We all have but one life to live and everyone in a sense wants to 'have it all'. To accept permanent exclusion from a way of being which is constantly, tantalizingly visible to us is surely contrary to human nature.

Nevertheless, only a small minority actually dare risk the censure and ridicule that comes to those who step outside their own gender universe. We can perhaps partly answer the question of what might motivate such risk-taking by considering why it should be that – in our own time and culture – cross-dressing seems to hold particular appeal for men.

In 'Fetishism' I described how, at the end of the eighteenth century, men in the West renounced the right to decorate or ornament themselves, fencing themselves into an extremely limited universe of meaning, behaviour and stylistic possibility. The limitations of this universe are especially obvious when it comes to dress and adornment but such stylistic restriction is only the most identifiable part of a greater impoverishment; from the Industrial Revolution onwards men have excluded themselves from all that is *charming* – that which possesses symbolic potency and allure.

The male transvestite – temporarily throwing off his shackles of 'manhood' – opens a door marked 'Off Limits' and enters a universe rich in all the things that his masculine universe lacks. These are of course precisely those things that 'real men' strive to dismiss as insignificant ('woman's things', 'fashion', 'trifles'), and great effort is put into maintaining this fiction. But despite all this the appeal of the charming can prove irresistible and there are only two means – both 'perversions' – by which the charming can be re-encountered from within this frustrating situation: fetishism and transvestism.

But didn't the Unisex Revolution change all this? To a point, perhaps, but when all is said and done, it is actually a very limited point. True, the last few decades have seen a phenomenal rise in 'men's wear' and at the same time a flowering of lifestyle magazines for men like *Arena*, *Esquire* and *GQ*, which feature a substantial amount of male fashion. And it is also true that our society has come to accept male pop stars from Bowie to Prince who dress and behave in ways that would have baffled and appalled our Victorian predecessors.

But all this aside, if you compare the sartorial and adornment possibilities on offer to Joe Public with those available to Jane Public it is readily apparent that, as far as dress is concerned, it is *women* rather than men who have benefited most from the Unisex Revolution. Today women in jeans, butch leather motorbike jackets and Dr Marten boots raise few eyebrows, but it would be another story for a man to go for a drink with his mates dressed in a skirt and stilettos. In a way, *most* women today are transvestites but it is only the male→female cross-dresser who is labelled as such and who bears the opprobrium of such classification. It is interesting to speculate on why this should have happened. Perhaps the reason hinges on the presumption that it is 'normal' for women to want to be more like men while it remains suspect for men to covet anything in the (by implication) 'inferior' woman's realm.

But whatever the reason, the fact remains that our definition of masculinity remains highly restrictive and this continues to make the grass look greener on the other side of the fence. If our culture should ever accept the degree of female→male appropriation which, in reverse, is increasingly taken for granted, then the future of transvestism as a specifically recognized activity might come to be in doubt.

This does not, however, seem a very likely prospect. However enlightened he may be, today's New Man shows no inclination to dress like Prince. Indeed, the New Man seems determined to achieve a degree of blandness and invisibility that even Old Man would have found worrying. No, the Great Masculine Renunciation is still very much with us and, accordingly, the future of transvestism seems assured.

In *Vested Interests: Cross-Dressing and Cultural Anxiety* Marjorie Garber argues that any culture – our own included – benefits greatly from the excursions that transvestites make across gender divides. Most obviously, it is the transvestite who provides the most telling and undeniable demonstration of the constructedness of gender identity.

But Garber's claim that 'there can be no culture without the transvestite' goes much further than this:

> For me . . . one of the most important aspects of cross-dressing is the way in which it offers a challenge to easy notions of binarity, putting into question the categories of 'female' and 'male', whether they are considered essential or constructed, biological or cultural. The current popularity of cross-dressing as a theme in art and criticism represents, I think, an undertheorized recognition of the necessary critique of binary thinking, whether particularized as male and female, black and white, yes and no, Republican and Democrat, self and other, or in any other way.[6]

I think I see what Garber is getting at and I like her model – the idea that the 'third term' of gender intervenes, confounds and disrupts. What I disagree with is her presumption that it is the transvestite who represents this 'third term' of gender. For like the transsexual, the transvestite operates *within* the system: s/he is no revolutionary.

Both the transsexual and the transvestite are the ultimate gender conservatives, preserving yesterday's definitions of 'femininity' and 'masculinity' against the onslaught of change. (Thereby, by the way, residing in the same time-warp which the fetishist inhabits.) To switch from one gender universe to the other (the transsexual) or to appropriate that gender universe which is contrary to one's own biology (the transvestite) is not in any way to challenge the existing constructions of 'masculinity' and 'femininity'. Indeed, both the transvestite and the transsexual have a vested interest in preserving the status quo.

To me, the truly 'disruptive' individual – the real 'third term' – is someone who shuns the established definitions of gender and who seeks to invent something new to put in their place. Masculinity and femininity are today bankrupt and grid-locked – too politicized to offer creative possibility. Switching them around or blending them into a cocktail is as pointless an exercise as rearranging the deck chairs on the *Titanic*. To see how a 'third term' of gender might open out in Garber's terms 'a space of possibility, structuring and confounding culture', we must leave behind the transvestite and the transsexual and check out the angel.

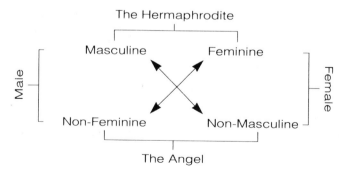

This diagram is an example of a device called 'the semiotic square', which was invented by the French linguist A. J. Greimas. As I understand it, its function is to show how meaning derives from various sets of opposites. While quite probably risking misinterpretation of Greimas' original ideas, to my eyes this diagram offers a concise and stimulating summary of our discussion of gender identity.

In the vertical relationship of the masculine and the non-feminine or that of the feminine and the non-masculine I see the process by which gender roles are constructed: the non-feminine and the non-masculine are the raw materials from which the edifices of masculinity and femininity are fabricated. The transsexual's journey is between these two, upper poles of opposition while the transvestite – the hermaphrodite – simultaneously embraces both of these conditions. At the bottom of the diagram, the angel straddles the 'raw', unconstructed poles of the non-feminine and the non-masculine, exalting in a composite of that which it is not; magically transforming a double negative into a positive.

The use of the term 'angel' may take many by surprise. Traditional angels – straddling another polarity, heaven and earth – are presumed to be 'sexless' in both senses of the word: they possess neither gender nor desire. But let us defy tradition and consider the possibility of a libidinal but un-gendered angel. Or, to be more precise, a creature which possesses sexual desire but is unconstrained and undefined by the established constructions of the masculine and the feminine. This, surely, is Marjorie Garber's true 'third term' of gender – that which is sufficiently estranged from the binary status quo to confound and disrupt.

Obviously I am talking about the kind of person who is usually described as 'androgynous'. But if you look up 'androgynous' or 'androgyne' in the dictionary the word offered as a synonym is 'hermaphrodite', implying a simple fusion of the masculine and the feminine. Why I like Greimas' diagram (and the term 'angel') is that it places us so squarely within the domain of the as yet undefined. For unlike the hermaphrodite, the angel exists within a universe that still awaits construction – an uncharted territory which contains within it ways of being which have yet to be labelled and which therefore open new doors of possibility.

Of course nothing, not even this angelic realm, is without a history. Throughout Western, Christian art one finds visual representations of heavenly angels that appear to point towards the possibility of a 'third term' of gender – a fusion of the non-feminine and the non-masculine. It is, however, in modern times and in a stridently secular context that we encounter the angel in more attainable forms.

David Bowie's wondrous creations of Ziggy Stardust and Aladdin Sane were universally described as 'androgynous' but in retrospect we can appreciate the inaccuracy of this classification. Ziggy and Aladdin were never fusions of existing masculine and feminine gender identities. They were not 'effeminate' in any true sense of the term, because their imagery didn't derive from either present or past feminine styles.

Transformed into these characters Bowie wasn't a 'man in a frock' and accordingly their place of origin was not of this planet. Like Frank-N-Furter in *The Rocky Horror Show*, Ziggy and Aladdin came from some distant erotic galaxy but unlike the Transylvanian transsexual in laddered fishnets and corset, they inhabited and celebrated the positive identity which can only result from the collision of the double negatives of the *not*-feminine and the *not*-masculine.

Having resided amongst the angels, Bowie eventually chose to fall to earth but the territory of a 'third term' of gender possibility that he initially explored has been visited by a steady stream of pop stars ever since. Marc Bolan, Sweet, Gary Glitter, Lou Reed, Bootsy Collins, Kiss, the New York Dolls, Alice Cooper, Boy George and Prince have all at times made the trip from the masculine to the angelic. (Because the universe of the feminine has become increasingly less defined in the last few decades it is more difficult to identify a similar list of (biologically) female angels, but Grace Jones, Siouxsie Sue, Annie Lennox, Madonna, k. d. lang and Sinéad O'Connor deserve our consideration.)

It is, however, amongst the more anonymous membership of the Scene that one finds such alternative possibilities of gender practised as well as preached. While the Scene contains its fair share of transsexuals and transvestites it is chock-a-block with angels. For such individuals, masculinity and femininity as traditionally constructed hold little appeal. The objective is to not look back – or even sideways.

As with Ziggy, Aladdin and so many of their descendants, this avoidance of established masculine and feminine styles has often been achieved by means of an aesthetic which is suitably 'far out' and 'futuristic' in terms of materials and garment/adornment styles. Or, alternatively, like the punks before them, many of the angels who inhabit the Scene have employed a 'modern primitive' iconography to point towards gender identities which exist outside Western culture. (If only in the angels' own mythologies of 'the primitive'.)

But while angelic tendencies within the Scene may be most obviously aesthetic it would be a mistake to assume that this is the end of the story. Beyond and yet encoded within these non-masculine/non-feminine appearances, a new way of being is also taking shape. Central to this is a radical reappraisal of the significance of biological gender. While the transsexual and the transvestite remain entrapped and ultimately defined by their genitals, the angel – truly convinced that gender is a fabrication and seeking to explore the full ramifications of this fact – proposes that what you have between your legs isn't a defining feature of who you are and what you can create of yourself.

For the angel, gender is a universe of being – a system of behaviours, symbolism and meaning – which is a DIY creation rather than the product of either chromosomes or surgical skill. Your genitals and the hormones that flow through your veins may not be an irrelevance but neither are they that which ultimately defines and limits identity.

Running parallel to and supporting this downgrading of the genitals as the essence of gender is the Scene's insistence that sexual experience need not be defined by copulation. Just as the angel points towards new possibilities of gender, the Scene as a whole points towards new possibilities of sexuality. In both instances the binary status quo (male/female, sex/not sex) is challenged and in the process invigorated.

May the Third Force be with you.

TANYA/HAMISH

Hamish, what do you do?

I'm a bondage and other leather items maker.

Tanya?

I'm a nanny. I've been doing it for two years now and I get a lot of
satisfaction out of it.

HOUSK

HAMISH

HOUSK

TANYA

HOUSK	When did you both become aware of your interest in bondage and S/M?
HAMISH	Well, my earliest memory is of being chained to a jetty by older boys when I was fourteen.

HOUSK	Did you enjoy it?
HAMISH	Yes. It was funny.
TANYA	I suppose I was fifteen or sixteen when I wanted to tie up my boyfriend. I'd thought about these things when I was younger but I didn't start trying them out until I became sexually active with men and women.

HOUSK	What role does it play in your life?
TANYA	It varies greatly. When we first met it was quite often, but then I broke my leg and we didn't do it at all. Now it's fairly regular again. We go off and on, like with our genital piercings. We'll take them out for a while, then put them back. If we're hot we'll take them out just for a particular sex session — we can get wild and we don't want to rip anything.

HOUSK	Can you describe what S/M does for you?
HAMISH	First off, I look at it more as pleasure and pain than sadomasochism. I like being tied up and teased rather than hurt. Tanya might crouch over my face, just out of reach of my tongue, and, because I'm firmly

restricted, I can't do anything. I'm not really into getting whipped, it would damage my tattoos, but Tanya likes a bit of a paddle.

I must admit I go through periods of wanting heavy abuse, usually when I

TANYA

get depressed or angry. It helps kick me out of it. If I find myself in one of those moods I'll deliberately piss Hamish off because I know he'll be rough with me and then I can relax.

So it's a release for you?

Definitely. Lately I haven't been at all well balanced emotionally.

The accident with my leg took away most of my self-confidence. I mean,

I've travelled all over the world on my own and never been afraid, and now I am. I don't like it.

HOUSK   Do you still need women?

TANYA   I haven't had any female partners since I came to England. I still have many female friends who I'm quite physical with, which I enjoy because I still like women's bodies more than men's. I've been faithful to Hamish and I'm quite happy about that as I'd been rather promiscuous before. I really love him dearly.

HAMISH   As far as I'm concerned we're together for life.

HOUSK   What turns you both on most?

HAMISH   Aesthetically, I like straps and buckles . . . bondage. The thing is that, since I make and deal with this equipment all day long, I'm a bit jaded. I think Tanya gets more excited.

TANYA   Restriction's what turns me on because I like to fight against it but it has to be done properly or I'll get out of it and then tell Hamish 'Fuck you!' I do play rough. Sometimes I'll just throw Hamish on his face and take him from behind, but I have to be more gentle then.

HOUSK   It sounds as if there's no defined role you each play.

HAMISH   That's right. If one of us needs or feels like a particular scene, that's what we'll do.

TANYA   Personally, I go through a big orgasm denial. I won't allow myself to come for weeks so that it's stronger when I do. If I masturbate and come a lot I get blasé about it, so self-denial really works for me . . . I also like suffocation techniques. I don't mean strangulation but having the air restricted through my nose and mouth. It puts me in an altered state. I like having my face pushed into a pillow so I can breathe, but only with difficulty. It helps me to focus on my genitals.

What are you searching for in this big orgasm? **HOUSK**

Pleasure! The feeling just taking over until I can't think. **TANYA**

I like to bury my face in Tanya's cunt, sort of back to the womb but better. **HAMISH**

We also use a lot of videos, water-sports and masturbation.

I'm restricting his level of wanking because we're trying for a baby and **TANYA**

his usual twice daily is not conducive to a high sperm count. I'll tell you

what, I also really love pornography. Especially if it's really hard S/M or

piercing, you know, extremely violent.

SEXUAL HEALING

The Scene is a place where angels can openly experiment with new gender identities – overriding the limitations of 'the masculine' and 'the feminine', transforming gender from problem to possibility.

The Scene is a place where the gridlocked battle of the sexes is being blithely sidestepped by placing the dynamics of sexual power within the non-gendered framework of Top-Active/Bottom-Passive.

The Scene is a place where the meaning of 'pleasure' is being re-evaluated and liberated. For some, this is a matter of contrasting or combining pleasure with pain. For others, it is a broadening of the parameters of pleasure so that all manner of tactile – often non-genital – sensations become a desirable end in themselves.

The Scene is a place where 'perverse lingering' is being stripped of its negative connotations and celebrated as a constructive, positive alternative to the dead-end of 'instant gratification'. Whether it is achieved by means of fetishism, exhibitionism, voyeurism, bondage, S/M, dramatic role-playing or simply the sharing of fantasies, the objective remains the same – experiencing that which the casual and the hurried is incapable of providing.

The Scene is a place where people are exploring the possibility of sexual experience as a viable route to expanded consciousness, spiritual enlightenment and ecstasy.

We touched on this idea in 'Pleasure and Pain' when considering the possible objectives of S/M. It would be a mistake, however, to give the impression that only S/M offers possibilities of transcendence. Mark Thompson's collection *Leatherfolk* is packed full of essays that propose an intrinsic link between all manner of radical sex practices and the spiritual.

For example, Ganymede in his essay 'Sacred Passages and Radical Sex Magic' explores the transcendent possibilities of ritualized body piercing, while Joseph W. Bean considers 'The Spiritual Dimensions of Bondage', elucidating how 'moments of complete equilibrium may turn to ecstasy'[1] and identifying the 'psychospiritual dynamics' of different bondage situations. And Dianna Vesta, in 'Fantasy, Fetish, and the Goddess' proposes that the power of the dominatrix should be likened to that of the female deities of the ancient earth religions.

Indeed, the whole of the concluding section of *Leatherfolk* is concerned with 'the spirit and the flesh'. Although most of these essays have been written by gays and lesbians, they point towards an all-encompassing theory of sexuality. Helpfully and ecumenically, rising above divisions of sexual orientation or practice, a more fundamental division is drawn between those who approach sex in a hurried, casual, mindless and recreational way and those who spurn immediate pleasures and, in such 'lingering', seek a route to ecstasy. In other words, the real divide is between sex as an end in itself and sex as a means — a vehicle of transcendence, a route to ecstasy in the true sense of the term.

'Erotic ecstasy' is a difficult concept for many of us. Our era has debased 'ecstasy' into a chemical experience most readily identified with scenes of robotic dancing, and more likely to generate numbness than enlightenment. Moreover, all our established religions look with disdain on any equation of sexual and ecstatic experience, insisting that such a state is achievable only by denial rather than indulgence.

This is not true, however, of the Tantric traditions of the Far East. According to Ajit Mookerjee and Madhu Khanna's *The Tantric Way*, this system of personal realization is distinguished by the fact that it is 'not a withdrawal from life, but the fullest possible acceptance of our desires, feelings and situations as human beings'.[2] Indeed, Tantra specifically identifies and celebrates sexual experience as 'a pathway for opening the realities of the cosmos, pointing towards the oneness of the finite and the infinite'.[3]

We should not be tempted to equate Tantra and the Scene too closely. Tantra's 'sexo-yogic disciplines' are but one facet of its complex programme for personal development. More typically, the Tantrika uses the repetition of verbal mantras, meditation on visual yantras or non-sexual yoga as a means of achieving spiritual development. While popular mythology has it that Tantric beliefs were simply a good excuse for an orgy, this was never actually the case. Tantra never denied the spiritually enhancing possibilities of sexual experience but neither did it accord such experience a central or essential place in its programme for personal fulfilment. This cannot be said of the Scene (provided of course that we define 'sex' more broadly than simply the act of copulation).

But while Tantra and the Scene are hardly one and the same thing, their sexual philosophies do repay comparison. Both use the structure of ritual and the potency of symbolism to locate sexual experience within some extraordinary domain. Both seek to find in sex something more than just a 'good time', shunning immediate, easy pleasure in the pursuit of that which has depth and resonance; 'lingering' to accomplish a build-up of sexual charge so as to catapult the participant into a higher level of consciousness. Both can produce a dramatic focusing of psychic energies. Both frame sexual experience within a world view concerned with fulfilment in the broadest sense while recognizing the erotic as a viable path to such fulfilment.

If the Scene's belief in transcendence via radical sex is sincere then it adds another important dimension to our discussion. Thus far I have suggested various ways in which Scene sex may offer constructive solutions to the crises of sexuality and gender that confront our society as a whole. Here, one would be proposing radical, alternative sexuality as a possible solution to another crisis that confronts our present era – that of spiritual impoverishment.

Can it really be true that people tying each other up, whipping each other, dressing up in fetish gear and so forth can activate well-springs of cosmic energy? It may seem unlikely but if we are prepared to accept that Tantra's sexo-yoga disciplines can provoke spiritual awakening, why shouldn't those who today indulge in 'ritual sex magic' open spiritual as well as erotic vistas too?

The case is perhaps made most eloquently by Mark Thompson himself in his introduction to *Leatherfolk*:

The idea that radical sexuality has spiritual value is a difficult one for most people to grasp. Many leatherfolk reject the thought as well, confusing spirituality with religiosity and its condemning institutions. Few, however, would dismiss the transcendent moments they've experienced through intense sexual ritual. For leather play is also about permitting ecstasy to enter our lives. The enhanced physical, visual, and aural sensations of radical sex ritual allow for a transportation of self, or awareness of self, beyond normal everyday reference. Leatherfolk often speak about vivid out-of-mind-and-body experiences. As they know, *surrender* is one of the most important and necessary elements of their play – a surrender of fear, inhibition, and ego to some deeper, unrecognized state within. Ecstatic revelation: this, by any other name, is spiritual.[4]

In a 1965 BBC television documentary, Malcolm Muggeridge commented with harsh sarcasm on 'The Religion of Sex' which had sprung up in the swinging sixties, noting that 'The new evangel is joyously proclaimed: to die in the spirit and be reborn in the flesh'. And his concern wasn't misplaced. While some of the hippies might have attempted a fusion of the erotic and the spiritual, from the early sixties to the present day the feeling has been that such a partnership is impossible, if not downright absurd. Despite hopeful allusions to 'sexual ecstasy' and 'cosmic turn-ons', pop sex's recreational imperative was always too locked into immediate, hedonistic pursuits to make the flesh anything but the spirit's all-conquering opponent.

It would seem, therefore, that the Scene's and the leatherfolk's pursuit of the spirit in the flesh marks a moment of historical importance. Whether radical sex can actually accomplish the degree of transcendence aspired to by its proponents is perhaps less important than the fact that it is being attempted. And such attempts could not come at a more opportune moment. We live in astoundingly, worryingly mean-spirited times. Has there, I wonder, ever been an era in all of human history when meaning, value and vision have been in such short supply? It is easy to scoff at the notion of 'sex magic' but can we as a spiritually bankrupt culture afford to do so?

TRUDY/STUART

HOUSK   Stuart, what do you do?

STUART I'm currently Chief Engineer for a breakfast TV franchise.

HOUSK   Trudy, how about you?

TRUDY   I'm an artist who works with virtual reality and sex . . . trying to link fine art

with computers.

When did you first become aware of S/M and that it worked for you? **HOUSK**

It was back in 1978 when I got my first PVC bed boots. **TRUDY**

Good question. I first became aware of it courtesy of *Penthouse* **STUART**
magazine. So about the same time Trude became aware I was finding
my own way, albeit second-hand. It was a superbly photographed
bondage feature called 'My Funny Valentine' and from that moment on I
never stopped, the effect was immediate and powerful . . . turned me on
like never before. Funny thing is my previous experience of this was
absolutely zero, so where my instant love of it came from, God only
knows.

When you and Trudy practise S/M what does it do for you? **HOUSK**

It provides a much more profound sense of loving and giving. People **STUART**
imply or imagine all sorts of awful things when they speak about S/M but
it isn't like that, it's sexual magic.

It's fun, too. We have a laugh with it because it can be serious or funny at **TRUDY**
the same time. You need to be totally open and trusting with the other
person.

You touched on the subject of sexual magic. What do you mean by **HOUSK**
that?

I had a whole weekend once where I was so spaced by the out-of-body **TRUDY**
experience of it that I needed my hand held just to cross the street.

Do you consider that a spiritual experience? **HOUSK**

Yes, it's a leaving of the body. I can get to a stage where the body isn't **TRUDY**
enough and I transcend it.

Do you maintain rigid roles or do you switch? **HOUSK**

We're both switchers. We're lucky, we've managed not to be in the **STUART**
same frame of mind at the same time yet.

TRUDY   Can you imagine! We both come out of the wardrobe with submissive gear on – 'oops, try again'.

STUART   The transition of roles is a slow one over a period of days or even weeks.

TRUDY   It also depends on what's happening in our lives. If Stuart is under a lot of pressure at work he likes to be submissive and, if I feel I have an important project on, I need to be aggressive so I become dominant.

HOUSK   When you're being submissive, Stuart, what are you getting from it?

STUART Well, now we're back to our spiritual quest . . . a heightened state of awareness. In my opinion this is only possible if it includes love. I don't think you can have a really satisfying S/M relationship without it.

HOUSK Is this spiritual quest the same whether you're dominant or submissive?

STUART It's certainly more apparent when you're being submissive but, as a dominant, you need to be aware of where you're taking your partner; then it can become a healing experience.

TRUDY	Definitely. Sometimes in a particular scene you can bring up emotions from the past that you needed to express but were unable to at the time and that can be very moving.
HOUSK	What part does S/M play in your lives?
STUART	We're full-time lovers and S/M is just a part of that.
TRUDY	It's full time in my art, though.
STUART	We actually have a very conventional sex life nineteen bonks out of twenty, but then . . .
HOUSK	All hell breaks loose?
TRUDY	Yes, it's Christmas! We first met at an S/M club and it all happened very quickly. At the time Stuart lived a long distance away but whenever we did see each other we'd practise S/M which was wonderful. Now that we live together it's eased off slightly and we tend to make love more regularly and have the S/M as cream on top of the cake.
HOUSK	Do you find conventional love-making as satisfying?
TRUDY	Depends. If we did S/M all the time it would get boring and vice versa, so we switch back and forth to keep things lively. It stays fresh that way, sort of like laundering your love life, because if you have any little aggressions with each other it's an ideal way to bring them out.
HOUSK	You mean in a safe, constructive way?
TRUDY	Yes, it's structured and controlled, so if either of us wants to stop at any time we can and have done. Also we tend to find the humour in it, which defuses anger, and we have to concentrate very hard on keeping

If either of us wants to stop at any time we can

serious or we discover ourselves collapsing with laughter at crucial moments. Stuart once put me in this really wonderful chastity belt, stainless steel, and then I wanted to get out to go to the loo. Well, what happens?

Stuart only loses the bloody keys and we end up with me stretched
across a table while he tries to cut me out with a huge saw—

—I've got the back of the belt clamped in this huge vice on the table and   **STUART**
Trude's bum is sticking up in the air while I saw away furiously.

It's happened more than once. I was locked into a tight slave's outfit one   **TRUDY**
night and went to bed in it. I woke up feeling constricted by it, I must have
swollen in my sleep, but when I asked Stuart to remove it he couldn't find

the keys so there he was, filing away again at three in the morning.

STUART   The moral to this story is buy good padlocks and make sure the key's in easy reach.

HOUSK   Any last words on S/M?

STUART   It's grossly misunderstood.

TRUDY   There's so much prejudice based on ignorance and fear—

STUART   —Fear of people's individual sexuality.

TRUDY   Don't knock it till you've tried it.

Radical sex practices may have the potential for spiritual awakening but, like all sex, if engaged in for the wrong reasons and with the wrong attitude, they can also be soul destroying. As the Scene has grown into a huge financial industry there has been a tendency to focus PR efforts upon the chic and the cheerful while sweeping any hint of problems in the Scene under the carpet. From the moment when Housk Randall and I began work on this book we resolved not to let *Rituals of Love* become compromised by this tendency. While we recognized that any critical reflections on the Scene might be exploited by elements within the media we also felt that such a blinkered approach would be irresponsible.

And counter-productive. Housk and I believe that the daring experimentation and openness which exists within the Scene offers possible ways out of the stupefied, frustrated mess that characterizes our modern society as a whole. But for any account of the Scene to be useful in this way it is necessary to distinguish between that which is positive and constructive and that which, in its negativity, can only obscure and inhibit personal progress. We also recognized that making such a distinction would never be easy.

The problem is, of course, that the very nature of the Scene places it outside the scope of traditional categorizations of the good, the bad and the ugly. One would not, for example, find much use for Freudian or post-Freudian definitions of 'perversity' or 'pathological behaviour' as these characterize just about everyone within the Scene and just about all of their radical sex practices as unhealthy. We then considered using 'extreme' fetishistic, Sub/Dom or S/M activities as a dividing line between the constructive and the destructive.

Immediately, of course, we faced the question 'How extreme is extreme?' but, just as significantly, we found ourselves recognizing that we knew individuals from the Scene whose radical sex practices could only be categorized as 'extreme' but whose objectives seemed valid and whose psychospiritual good health seemed evident.

Perhaps more promising, we thought, would be to apply the notion of 'sexual addiction', which has gained currency as a term to describe the behaviour of someone who compulsively engages in casual sex. Such promiscuity is not commonly found in the Scene but we wondered if amongst radical sex practitioners other forms of sexual compulsion might be identified. For example, we both knew of people who seemed to be desperately, frantically indulging in ever-more complicated, precisely defined and occasionally even dangerous sexual activities, while never apparently reaching their objective or questioning whether something more than technical elaboration was required to reach those objectives.

While such discussions brought Housk and I tantalizingly close to a point where a line could be drawn between positive and negative radical sex behaviour, we were at the same time sidetracked by the Sexual Recovery movement's own lack of rigour in defining 'compulsive' sexual behaviour. Like established psychoanalytic notions of 'perversity', the sexual addiction theorist's tendency to equate sexual/erotic preoccupation with the compulsive or addictive seemed to require that virtually *everyone* within the Scene (including Housk and me) sign up immediately with Sexaholics Anonymous. In essence, it seemed to us the Sexual Recovery movement's core criterion for distinguishing between 'good' and 'bad' sex was simply quantitative – masturbation once a day is OK but masturbate ten times a day and you've officially 'got a problem'. But what about five times a day? And what if the ten-times-a-day person is actually having a good time, aside from a bit of genital soreness and muscle fatigue?

At least Housk and I were now clearer about what it was we were looking for: a qualitative rather than quantitative demarcation. We considered all the radical sex activities. Were there certain specific Sub/Dom, S/M or fetishistic activities that were intrinsically psychologically destructive? We couldn't identify any. We seemed to have come to a dead end when suddenly I was reminded of a remark Housk had made during one of our earliest discussions: 'First you need to build a good relationship and *then* you can play games and experiment. It seems to me that some people in the Scene have got this the wrong way around.'

Did this imply, I wondered, that 'good', constructive, positive radical sex can only occur within the context of a stable, long-term relationship? Housk: 'No, not necessarily. I think what I was trying to say was that in my view radical sex – like any sex – must be fundamentally about people *relating to each other as people*. And that, without this, all the rituals, techniques, equipment in the world won't actually get you anywhere.'

We realized we couldn't bypass the central issue any longer. And, in fact, it had been there all along, in the title that Housk had thought up for our book.

In the most remarkable and touching of all the essays in *Leatherfolk*, 'Living in Leather: An Inner Journey', Gabrielle Antolovich describes how, as a leather dyke, she broke out of her self-constructed 'paradise of hell', put her 'dark shadowy side' into perspective and discovered true love. Antolovich's journey begins with her as:

> A panther stalking its prey. I could feel the darkness take over my heart like a slow fog on a cold winter evening. What was taking me? I wanted to be mean, tough, vicious, revengeful, cruel, and cold. The women I found fed the dark side with their desires to be taken and beaten and told what to do.[5]

But realizing that this wasn't actually providing real satisfaction, Antolovich began a painful microscopic examination of herself, her past and her
dis-ease. However, it was the arrival of 'the sweetest woman I had ever dared to
experience', which ultimately invigorated this self-examination. She didn't want
to 'contaminate' her visitor – 'I even *liked* her; my heart bounced giddily just to
know she existed' – and together they explored the darkness lurking in their
hearts. From this process, a profound insight:

The dark side is not so much the whips and chains, the black leather, or the attitudes: it
is the unresolved pains from the past being twisted into some kind of sexual desire. I
want to be free from that twist.[6]

Cleansed, healed, renewed, Antolovich and her sweet Queen go on to build a
new and special 'dungeon' – 'with bits of each of our fantasies, with secret
entrances and exits, and a room full of daisy chains and a bed full of roses'.[7]

Leather roses. The moral of this wonderful fairy tale is not only that
kinkiness needs love to cleanse it of its sticky residues and vampiric cruelty but
also that love can indeed arrive dressed in a leather catsuit and carrying a whip.
For, like desire, love is a chameleon which must accommodate itself to history.

PHOTOGRAPHER'S POSTSCRIPT

It is early afternoon when I arrive at the home of a couple who have agreed to be photographed for *Rituals of Love*. These two are long-standing members of the sexual underground whom I have known as personal friends for many years. They welcome me and help to carry my equipment into their flat.

We begin with some fairly straightforward portraits, which we do in the garden between bursts of rain. The mood is casual and relaxed. This stage completed, we have a cup of coffee and discuss what to do next. As with all of the couples I've photographed for this book I am eager to let them decide what and how much of their personal sexuality they want to expose to my camera.

This particular couple's main interest is bondage and S/M and they propose to enact a favourite fantasy in the 'dungeon', which occupies their spare room. I set up my camera and lights and gradually a complex erotic ritual unfolds. I am witnessing and recording a scene of great intensity which after about half an hour I begin to find disturbing. Things seem to be getting out of control and I'm worrying that it is my presence – and the camera's – that is provoking what appears to be an excessively violent and cruel scenario.

I'm on the verge of calling a halt and leaving when suddenly the 'victim' of this ritual turns to me, smiling, and asks if I have all the shots I need because, if so, would I kindly leave the room as they are both feeling very excited and would like to make love. I wait in the kitchen turning over in my mind what has just happened – how even a long-standing member of the Scene like myself can misinterpret things. Love and mutual respect can lie at the core of that which appears to be cruel and heartless.

The first time I ever went to a fetish club I saw a woman who was naked except for a rubber hood which covered her head. She was being led by a leather-clad man who was holding a chain attached to a large ring through her clitoris. I was horrified. A friend, noticing that I was upset, said, 'Don't be so fast to judge what you see. Not everything here is as it seems.'

While this is true of life in general, it is especially relevant to the Scene. I hope that those of you who see the pictures I have taken will realize that things are not always what they seem – in particular, there is more love here than meets the eye.

This is not to say that everything is perfect in the land of the new rubber Oz. As in any cross-section of society there are givers and takers, the used and their abusers, those who find themselves and the unfortunate few who get hopelessly lost. But those who think that love, affection and mutual respect cannot exist within such 'perversity' are mistaken.

Photographers approach their work in many different ways. For some, it is technique that matters most – the subject matter may be almost irrelevant. Personally, I find it very difficult to photograph anything that I'm not passionate about. Nor do I want to be a 'hired gun': I need to be personally involved in what I'm recording. Since my childhood I have been fascinated by alternative approaches to sexuality and the erotic. After overcoming my initial misunderstanding of what goes on in the Scene I have come to realize that here is a world that shares this fascination.

More than this, at its best the Scene really is a place of tolerance, acceptance and mutual support. I am thankful to have been a part of this community. As a photographer I am grateful to those who have dared to reveal to my camera their most intimate practices and dreams.

NOTES

HOT MONOGAMY

1   Jean Baudrillard, *Seduction* (New World Perspectives, Montreal, 1990), p. 5.

2   Andrew Neil, 'Laid Bare: Unmasking Madonna' in the *Sunday Times Magazine*, 18 October 1992, p. 21.

3   Baudrillard, op. cit., p. 5.

4   Ibid.

FETISHISM

1   Karl Marx, *Capital: A Critique of Political Economy* (Modern Library, New York, 1906), p. 81.

2   Translated and quoted in Emily Apter, *Feminizing the Fetish: Psychoanalysis and Narrative Obsession in Turn-of-the-Century France* (Cornell University Press, Ithaca and London, 1991), p. 20.

3   Sigmund Freud, *The Standard Edition of the Complete Psychological Works* (ed. James Strachey), vol. 23 (The Hogarth Press, London, 1974), pp. 202–3.

4   In Apter, op. cit., p. 17.

5   *Relate: An Illustrated Journal of Correspondence*, vol. 4, no. 1.

6   Apter, op. cit., p. 80.

7   J. C. Flugel, *The Psychology of Clothes* (The Hogarth Press, London, 1930), pp. 110–11.

8   *Fashion Weekly*, 12 November 1992, p. 13.

SEX AND POWER

1   Leopold von Sacher-Masoch, *Venus in Furs* (Blast Books, New York, 1989), p. 118.

2   Marquis de Sade, *The 120 Days of Sodom* (Grove Press, New York, 1966), pp. 250–1.

3   Terence Sellers, *The Correct Sadist* (Temple Press, Brighton, 1990), p. 17.

4   Sellers, ibid.

5   Pauline Reage, *The Story of O* (Corgi Books, London, 1985), p. 121.

6   Sacher-Masoch, op. cit., p. 134.

7   Sellers, op. cit., pp. 20–1.

8   Helen Henley, *Enter With Trumpets* (Atomage Publishing, London, 1982), pp. 12–13.

9   Jim E. Dickson, *The Story of Gerda* (Atomage Publishing, London, 1982), p. 15.

10   Dickson, ibid., p. 32.

11   *O* magazine, no. 8, p. 32.

12   Reage, op. cit., pp. 125–6.

PLEASURE AND PAIN

1   Sacher-Masoch, op. cit., p. 15.

2   Pat Califia, 'The Limits of the S/M Relationship, or Mr Benson Doesn't Live Here Any More', in Mark Thompson, *Leatherfolk* (Alyson Publications, Boston, 1991), p. 223.

3   Ibid., p. 232.

4   Ibid., pp. 229–30.

5   In Thompson, op. cit., p. 32.

6   Ibid., p. 38.

7   Ibid, p. 55.

8   Alex Kershaw, 'Love Hurts' in *Guardian Weekend*, 28 November 1992, p. 10.

9   Jon Savage, 'Sex and Martyrdom' in the *Observer*, February 1992, p. 51.

10   Kershaw, op. cit., p. 6.

11   Savage, op. cit., p. 50.

12   Ibid., p. 51.

13   Kershaw, op. cit., p. 10.

14   Ibid., p. 12.

GENDER PLAY

1   Philip Norman, 'Sexual Signals' in the *Guardian*, 24 July 1993, p. 8.

2   In Housk Randall, *Revelations* (Tim Woodward Publishing, London, 1993), p. 7.

3   Liz Hodgkinson, 'Altered States' in the *Guardian*, 14 June 1990, p. 17.

4   Marjorie Garber, *Vested Interests: Cross-Dressing and Cultural Anxiety* (Penguin Books, London, 1992), p. 101.

5   Ibid., p. 109.

6   Ibid., pp. 10–11.

SEXUAL HEALING

1   In Thompson, op. cit., p. 258.

2   Ajit Mookerjee and Madhu Khanna, *The Tantric Way* (Thames & Hudson, London, 1993), p. 9.

3   Ibid., p. 24.

4   In Thompson, op. cit., p. xix.

5   Ibid., p. 252.

6   Ibid., p. 256.

7   Ibid.

BIBLIOGRAPHY

Apter, Emily, *Feminizing the Fetish: Psychoanalysis and Narrative Obsession in Turn-of-the-Century France* (Cornell University Press, Ithaca and London, 1991)

Bataille, Georges, *Eroticism* (Marion Boyars, London, 1987)

——*The Story of the Eye* (Marion Boyars, London, 1979)

Baudrillard, Jean, *Seduction* (New World Perspectives, Montreal, 1990)

Binet, Alfred, 'Le fétichisme dans l'amour' in *Revue Philosophique*, no. 24 (1887), pp. 142–67 and 252–74

Bradbury, Dominic, 'Adventures in the Skin Trade' in *Fashion Weekly*, 12 November 1992

Brand, Clavel, *Fetish* (Luxor Press Ltd, London, 1970)

Bright, Susie, *Sexual Reality: A Virtual Sex World Reader* (Cleis Press Inc., San Francisco, 1992)

Califia, Pat, *Macho Sluts* (Alyson Publications, Inc., Boston, 1988)

Centurion's Whole Catalogue of the Exotic & Bizarre, The (Centurion Publications, USA, 1982)

Crosland, Margaret (ed.), *The Passionate Philosopher: a de Sade Reader* (Peter Owen, London, 1991)

Dickson, Jim E., *The Story of Gerda* (Atomage Publishing, London, 1982)

Flugel, J. C., *The Psychology of Clothes* (The Hogarth Press, London, 1930)

Freud, Sigmund, *The Standard Edition of the Complete Psychological Works* ed. James Strachey (The Hogarth Press, London, 1974)

Friday, Nancy, *My Secret Garden* (Quartet Books, London, 1980)

Gamman, Lorraine & Makinen, Merja, *Female Fetishism* (Lawrence & Wishart, London, 1994)

Garber, Marjorie, *Vested Interests: Cross-Dressing and Cultural Anxiety* (Penguin Books, London, 1992)

Gold, Herbert, 'The New Wave Makers' in *Playboy*, vol. 14, no. 10 (1967), pp. 128–37

Green, Jonathon, *It: Sex Since the Sixties* (Secker & Warburg, London, 1993)

Greimas, A. J., and Courtes, J. (eds), *Semiotics and Language: An Analytical Dictionary* (Indiana University Press, Bloomington, 1982)

Henley, Helen, *Enter With Trumpets* (Atomage Publishing, London, 1982)

Hodgkinson, Liz, 'Altered States' in the *Guardian*, 14 June 1990, p. 17

Kershaw, Alex, 'Love Hurts' in the *Guardian Weekend*, 28 November 1992, pp. 6–12

Kirk, Kris, and Heath, Ed, *Men in Frocks* (GMP, London, 1984)

Krafft–Ebing, Richard von, *Psychopathia Sexualis* (1886). Transl. Harry E. Wedeck (Putnam's, New York, 1965)

Kunzle, David, *Fashion and Fetishism* (George Prior Associated Publishers Ltd, London, 1982)

Leigh, Michael, *The Velvet Underground* (The Annihilation Press, London, 1991)

Madonna, *Sex* (Secker & Warburg Ltd, London, 1992)

Marx, Karl, *Capital: 'A Critique of Political Economy*, (Modern Library, New York, 1906)

McDowell, Colin, *Dressed to Kill* (Hutchinson, London, 1992)

Mookerjee, Ajit, and Khanna, Madhu, *The Tantric Way* (Thames & Hudson, London, 1993)

Neil, Andrew, 'Laid Bare: Unmasking Madonna' in the *Sunday Times Magazine*, 18 October 1992, pp. 18–23

Norman, Philip, 'Sexual Signals' in the *Guardian*, 24 July 1993, pp. 6–9

Paglia, Camille, *Sexual Personae* (Vintage Books, New York, 1991)

Polhemus, Ted, *Bodystyles* (Lennard Publishing, London, 1988)

Polhemus, Ted, and Procter, Lynn, *Fashion & Anti-Fashion: An Anthropology of Clothing and Adornment* (Thames & Hudson, London, 1978)

Randall, Housk, *Revelations* (Tim Woodward Publishing, London, 1993)

Reage, Pauline, *The Story of O* (Corgi Books, London, 1985)

——*The Story of O, Part II* (Corgi Books, London, 1985)

——*The New Story of O* (Nexus, London, 1992)

Rossi, William A., *The Sex Life of the Foot and Shoe* (Routledge & Kegan Paul, London, 1977)

Sacher-Masoch, Leopold von, *Venus In Furs* (Blast Books, New York, 1989)

Sade, Marquis de, *Justine: or The Misfortunes of Virtue* (Corgi Books, London, 1970)

——*The 120 Days of Sodom* (Grove Press, New York, 1966)

Savage, Jon, 'Sex and Martyrdom' in the *Observer*, February 1992, pp. 50–55

Sellers, Terence, *The Correct Sadist* (Temple Press, Brighton, 1990)

Smith, Bradley, *The American Way of Sex* (Gemini Smith, New York, 1978)

Smithfield, Arthur P., *Compulsive Sex Practices* (Academy Press, San Diego, 1970)

Steele, Valerie, *Fashion and Eroticism* (Oxford University Press, New York, 1985)

Talese, Gay, *Thy Neighbour's Wife: Sex in the World Today* (William Collins Sons & Co, London, 1980)

Thompson, Mark (ed.), *Leatherfolk: Radical Sex, People, Politics, and Practices* (Alyson Publications, Boston, 1991)

Various, 'The Games Singles Play' in *Newsweek*, 16 July 1973, pp. 32–6

Various, *I–D: The Sexuality Issue*, vol. 110, November 1992

Vassi, Marco, *Metasex, Mirth & Madness* (Penthouse Press, New York, 1975)

Vickers, Mike, 'A Day at the Races' in *O* Magazine, no. 8, pp. 31–5

Willie, *The Change* (Constance Enterprises, New Jersey, 1991)

Wolfe, Tom, 'The Boiler Room and the Computer' in *Mauve Gloves & Madmen, Clutter & Vine*, (Bantam Books, New York, 1977), pp. 166–71.